HOUSES DIVIDED

HOUSES DIVIDED

A Letter to the Churches of the USA on Church and State

MARILYNN KNOTT

Copyright © 2013 Marilynn Knott.

All rights reserved. No part of this book may be used or reproduced by any means, graphic, electronic, or mechanical, including photocopying, recording, taping or by any information storage retrieval system without the written permission of the publisher except in the case of brief quotations embodied in critical articles and reviews.

New Revised Standard Version Bible: Anglicized Edition, copyright 1989, 1995, Division of Christian Education of the National Council of the Churches of Christ in the United States of America. Used by permission. All rights reserved.

Archway Publishing books may be ordered through booksellers or by contacting:

Archway Publishing
1663 Liberty Drive
Bloomington, IN 47403
www.archwaypublishing.com
1-(888)-242-5904

Because of the dynamic nature of the Internet, any web addresses or links contained in this book may have changed since publication and may no longer be valid. The views expressed in this work are solely those of the author and do not necessarily reflect the views of the publisher, and the publisher hereby disclaims any responsibility for them.

Any people depicted in stock imagery provided by Thinkstock are models, and such images are being used for illustrative purposes only. Certain stock imagery © Thinkstock.

ISBN: 978-1-4808-0367-1 (sc)
ISBN: 978-1-4808-0368-8 (e)

Library of Congress Control Number: 2013919586

Printed in the United States of America

Archway Publishing rev. date: 11/11/2013

To Erwin Ned Knott and Karlanne Knott Harshman, my brother and sister in life and in Christ

CONTENTS

Acknowledgments..................................ix
Introduction 1
Chapter 1:   Of Church 11
Chapter 2:   Faith Fed, Not Fear Bound 20
Chapter 3:   Inclusive, Not Exclusive 25
Chapter 4:   Empathetic, Not Judgmental 31
Chapter 5:   Sharing, Not Hoarding................. 36
Chapter 6:   Sin 43
Chapter 7:   Of State............................. 58
Chapter 8:   Promote the General Welfare 63
Chapter 9:   Exploring the Other Purposes of the
             United States......................... 70
Chapter 10: Government and Productivity............. 80
Chapter 11: Commonly Held Values 86
Chapter 12: The Economy 89
Chapter 13: The Issues That Divide Us: Abortion....... 101
Chapter 14: The Issues That Divide Us: Guns 113
Chapter 15: The Issues That Divide Us: Immigration.... 120
Chapter 16: The Issues That Divide Us: Homosexuality.. 126
Chapter 17: Hear the Call 136
Afterword 141
Endnotes.. 143

ACKNOWLEDGMENTS

Where to start? The great cloud of witnesses that impacted my life—from family, teachers (both in public school and in church school), ministers and other church staff, coworkers, and friends—all deserve my gratitude for the many gifts they have given me in my formation. Besides grounding me in faith, my mother, Helen Philips Knott, gave me the genealogy bug, and my dad, Carl Warner Knott, by example mentored me in the art of storytelling. My brother, Erwin, is the salt of the earth and forces me to broaden my thinking all the time. My sister, Karlanne, is the best friend anyone could ever have. Between the two of them, I have been gifted with wonderful nieces, nephews, grandnieces, and –nephews, who are a source of great joy in my life.

There are so many people with whose paths my own crossed while working for the Department of Human Services. I cannot list them all or properly acknowledge their contributions to my development. Hopefully, they will see themselves herein on nearly every page. Ongoing friendships and support have been invaluable to me.

I particularly must acknowledge the people at Crown Heights Christian Church (Disciples of Christ), of which I have been a member for coming up on forty years, including the Hood Fellowship, my core support; the Mission Team, where actions speak louder than words; the First Sunday Book Club, where words mean a lot; and Friday Frolics, my source of pure fellowship.

Thanks to my dear friends Jackie Stinnett and Clarice Morrison, who carefully read the manuscript and gave me valuable suggestions and insights from both sides of the political spectrum. They held my hand and walked with me through my fears and doubts as I pursued this book. They also have been with me for decades in many of the perils and joys of life and spiritual growth.

The people who coordinate, teach, train, and inspire through the Commissioned Minister Training Program of the Christian Church in Oklahoma were most helpful in my ministry growth and development. At the time I participated, Jerry Black and Les Brown were the coordinators. Joe Jones was my theology teacher and graciously read a first draft of part of *Houses Divided*, giving good advice and counsel.

Bob Gardenhire, Curt Gruel, and Kay Morgan contributed to my spiritual development, as did my fellow participants on our three-year journey through HeartPaths Spirituality Center, where I received my certification as a spiritual director.

The sisters at the Christine Center in Wisconsin gave me just the unbiased reflection I needed to go forward with *Houses Divided* when I was questioning my plans.

I would be remiss if I did not thank Don Oliver of Do Fitness Gym, who had both nothing and everything to do with the book. After ten years of limping around with a horrid knee, I had it replaced with the hope of gaining a more active lifestyle. The rehab work I did on my own just was not enough. With my very biased opinion that personal trainers were for the rich and famous or super athletes wanting to reach a higher fitness level, I succumbed to his cajoling—*badgering* might be the better word—and learned what perseverance can do. While it did indeed get me in better physical shape, it also got me off my duff to write *Houses Divided*, which I had been trying to avoid. Actually, much of the writing took place in

INTRODUCTION

"To all God's beloved in the [USA], who are called to be saints: Grace to you and peace from God our Father and the Lord Jesus Christ" (Romans 1:7).[1] I am borrowing Paul's oft-used salutation to introduce this work not to draw from his solutions to the complex problems that confronted first-century Christians, but to suggest that his form of communication might be a good guide for twenty-first-century Christians in finding their own way. My purpose in writing is to deal with church and state issues with the intention of providing edification for the church that will lead to more probing dialogue within and among churches.

To help you understand my starting point, I want to briefly explain my conception of Paul's style. Paul was committed to the kingdom of God, as indeed was Jesus Christ. Paul posits that the kingdom of God was realized with Jesus through his death and resurrection and that the kingdom of God will not come to fulfillment until Jesus' return. In the meantime (that is, now) the followers of Jesus Christ are to live as fully involved citizens of the kingdom of God, actively engaged in the business of the kingdom. Citizens of the kingdom of God function under a covenant with two overarching provisions: to love God and to love our neighbors as we love ourselves.

The word *kingdom* is rather archaic for most of us today, even in countries where there is a king or queen. In all honesty, our language does not have the words to adequately describe God or the realm/domain over which God is God. We humans think in terms of space and place, or we think in terms of style of governance, none of which may apply to God. In Jewish tradition, the ultimate "kingdom" most likely brought images of King David. Jesus' use of the term was most likely meant to draw this comparison. After all, David was the person who led Israel out of being a tribal nomadic people into becoming a great world power at the time. Jesus' purpose was to take first-century Jews' thinking out of the sphere of Roman rule and to some extent Jewish legalism into an understanding that God was more than any human forms, structures, or processes. The connection between God and humans from the start of the relationship was covenantal, a sacred agreement not to be broken. Jesus' disciples where charged with the responsibility of passing on that legacy to all who followed, including us today, wherever we may find ourselves in space and time and governance. It was always associated with a community of faith. Today, we Christians call it the body of Christ with many diverse members bonded together in love.

Paul took that charge to heart. His letters illustrate his attempts to bring Christ's followers into the oneness of that covenantal relationship. The letters to the Corinthians are a good example. Some scholars believe the first letter was not the first and that the second letter may be a compilation of several letters[2]. As far as I know, we do not have any of the letters from the church in Corinth, but there obviously were some. The letters of Paul were not edicts reporting final decisions. They were conversation starters for people of diverse backgrounds to use to find the oneness that is bound by the love of God. Nor were the letters intended to start debates to see who could win a vote on who was right and who was wrong. They were part of a dialogue wrapped in prayer, studied through the scriptures, and filled with grace. They were designed to show Christians how to proceed in loving God and loving their neighbors in whatever space and time and governance they might find themselves.

Galatians 2 tells the story of such a conversation. Great controversy raised its ugly head even in the first century. What were they to do about the Gentiles? Should they be circumcised? Should they eat meat offered to idols? It was a messy discussion, and my guess is many small group meetings and letters went back and forth as they eventually worked out a compromise. They may have actually agreed to disagree for a while. What I found most interesting, though, even in all the back and forth of sometimes heated conversation, is that they found something that they all absolutely agreed on: to help the poor. They did not call a halt to being the one body of Christ until they figured out the Gentile issue. They kept working toward discernment while doing together the things they could agree on.

The themes have changed over the past two thousand years but the human need to parse meaning and meaningfulness continues. We still have great controversies over which we argue. But there is rarely an issue that exists that we cannot address in some way or another as the one body of Christ.

Perhaps part of the problem is that we have grown so accustomed to scripture and have prayed the same prayers for so long that we may not be opening ourselves to the fullness of relationship with God. A few years ago I recorded scripture related to a Bible study for a participant whose vision was failing and who could no longer read the written word. I found that I could record long passages of scripture with all the proper style, but when I got to the end of the assigned scripture, I could not necessarily tell you what I had read. It made me wonder if my comfort level with scripture was inhibiting new insights that would be even more beneficial to me. Because of this, I have chosen to use the word *nation* instead of *kingdom* throughout this writing. I admit that *nation* is as inadequate as kingdom and has as many distractions, particularly since it is often used to describe "the other" in the Bible. My hope is that by changing the word, I will be forced to really consider what it means in the context of Jesus' teachings. I hope also that will be helpful to you.

Steps toward Becoming One

The twentieth century here on earth saw the first steps of bringing the world as we know it to a common table. First, the League of Nations was formed in conjunction with World War I. The next attempt at coordinating nations came following World War II when the United Nations was initiated. We Christians, however, have had the challenge of bringing the world together to the same table for two thousand years with the caveat that the work was to be done through acts of love, not as the result of war.

Actually, of course, Jesus drew his commands from the ancient scriptures of the Hebrews:

Hear, O Israel: The Lord is our God, the Lord alone. You shall love the Lord your God with all your heart, and with all your soul, and with all your might. (Deuteronomy 6:4–5)

You shall love your neighbor as yourself: I am the Lord. (Leviticus 19:18b)

Thus God's desire for the rule of love was established early.

We also see God's intent expressed in the blessing of Abraham following his obedience to God regarding the offering of his son Isaac. God rescued Isaac from death and followed that with the blessing of Abraham, which included these words:

And by your offspring shall all the nations of the earth gain blessing for themselves, because you have obeyed my voice. (Genesis 22:18)

To me, this story illustrates that while God values our fidelity, God cares as much about how we love each other both as individuals and as groups. God thus set the stage for our relationships with other nations.

A Nation within Nations

I was born in Oklahoma and have lived here most of my life. Oklahoma is a unique state. It is the place where numerous Indian tribes were relocated as white settlement spread across our great land. Although the treatment the tribes experienced is a sad and shame-filled part of US history, I believe these tribes in many ways have been a blessing to me and the other nonnative citizens of Oklahoma. While several tribal headquarters are located in Oklahoma, members of the tribes may live all over the earth and still retain their tribal identity. Many American Indians are also a part of the nation of God.

As Christians we function somewhat like these indigenous people—as a nation within many other nations. While the nation of God cannot be defined by a specific place, we indeed have our own rituals, rules, and relationships. The US government recognizes religious organizations as a distinct type of entity, for example, by extending tax exemptions, because the organizations are considered to be providing services that also contribute to the common good.

As citizens of such a civil authority, we come under its governance—just as citizens of the nation of God come under God's authority. Within God's authority, we come under the command to be a blessing to all nations. Through God's grace and mercy, we can be a blessing to all nations.

Christians are, however, one of the most divided groups that exist in the United States today. I hear public policy ideas being credited to Christians that are totally foreign to me. Yet

I have experienced the sudden intake of breath followed by silence and a quick change of subject in my own family when I have stated ideas that I value but are obviously anathema to those around me.

My brother is a dedicated student of the Bible, as I try to be, and yet we share differing understandings of it. Over the past several years, probably since our mother died in 2007, we have gotten into the habit of talking on the phone most Saturday mornings. At first we did not talk about our faith so much, but over time we have grown through deep dialogues. We have found concepts on which we agree, concepts on which we are not that far apart, and concepts on which we disagree. I must say one of the byproducts of our discussions is that we have both been challenged to explore more deeply why we believe what we believe and to live what we believe. Our conversations could not take place were they not grounded in love. He is my brother, we have always loved each other and always will. That is a great place to start for all of us brothers and sisters in Christ.

I am also very close to my sister, but we rarely discuss theology. She lives her faith every day with everyone. She is an example that we should all emulate. She does love God with all her heart, and she loves her family, her neighbors, her coworkers, and strangers who might catch her attention. She is the one who calls me and says, "So-and-so needs prayers—her son is in trouble." I always add their names to my prayer list, but I also always find it amusing that one of the greatest prayer warriors of all times is calling me to pray. I do need to be called to prayer, however, for I can get too caught up in the language of faith and sometimes do not give enough attention to the source.

Thus, I will attempt in these pages to share my insights to start the conversations that I believe are needed: first, to fulfill Jesus' call that we are all to be one, and second, to explore how that might look as a nation within a nation among diverse peoples of faith. I, however, write with the second letter to the Corinthians echoing in my head. This is my first letter to you. I, like Paul, may have to write a follow-up, saying, "Let me try that again."

While Paul's activities for uniting Christ's followers have broad implications, I have only chosen two to explore regarding the issue of church and state today and will begin with them.

First, how does the nation of God relate to a nation that claims to be a government of the people, by the people, and for the people? The documentation of God found in the Bible is set in predemocracy lands.

Most often those lands are described as pagan, made up of people who worshiped other gods from which the Hebrews sought isolation in peace. Rome was actually progressive, as it functioned as a republic not unlike our government, although its senators and tribunes were not elected. Jesus, when asked about paying taxes, said, "Give therefore to the emperor the things that are the emperor's, and to God the things that are God's" (Matthew 22:21). What happens when we followers of Christ are the emperor? Pogo said it best: "We have met the enemy ... and he is us."[3] Whether we like it or not, we citizens of the United States do not have the luxury of pointing a finger at the other and crying foul. If we want to know what is wrong with the government in the United States, we need only look in the mirror.

We the people of the United States seem to have lost our collective focus. We are very much like the Israelites of old, wandering in the wilderness,[4] directionless, without a rudder. We put everything we can into a golden calf and are shocked to find that it is just a tarnished, powerless golden calf. I cannot tell you why this happened to us now. Perhaps the bombings on 9/11 showed us how vulnerable we are, but you can read various versions of the same story over and over in the scriptures. It seems we who call ourselves Christians have lost sight of whose we are. As a citizen of the United States it sure feels like we have no control over our government when powerful lobbyists wheel and deal our futures away. The common good is not so common anymore. Is it any wonder that gridlock results?

Second, how do we Christians, who cannot seem to agree on many things, share in a secular government that includes many people of other religions or no religion at all? We strongly resist theocracies that are not Christian, so we in turn must not demand our own theocracy. But how do we discern policies that are fair to all and protect everyone's religious rights?

In the history of God's people, it seems to me that we are most able to love and to be a blessing to each other when we are faith fed, not fear bound; inclusive, not exclusive; empathetic, not judgmental; and sharing, not hoarding.

Why Me?

Although my eighth grade teacher predicted that I would write a book someday, I have come to this task with much hesitation but with a fire in my belly that I cannot otherwise extinguish. I overheard the Bible being read from the womb. I have known no other way of life than one that involves a relationship with Jesus Christ. Actually, as a student of my own genealogy, I can tell you that five generations ago, my ancestor William Knott was one of the trustees who helped establish a Methodist Church in Pennsylvania. The chairs around my mother's table were purchased from my great-grandfather Philip's Presbyterian church in Arkansas.

That said, I spent thirty-five years of my life working as a public servant at the Oklahoma Department of Human Services. I started as a caseworker in 1969 during the onset of the Great Society, retiring in 2004 as the administrator of policy, planning and research when the phrase "faith-based initiatives" was in vogue. I believe in this country and the principles on which it was founded. I have walked the tightrope of the separation of church and state in practice as well as in theory. Since my retirement, I have obtained my credential as a commissioned minister in the Christian church (Disciples of Christ) and worked full-time for eight years as an assistant minister, seeing firsthand the failures and successes of both the church and the state in response to human need. My hope and prayer is that my sharing experiences and insights might be a catalyst for conversations on church and state among Christians and beyond.

Structure of This Book

To provide for a common faith foundation, the first part of this book briefly sketches the basic tenets of Christianity that, I believe, can be acknowledged by the vast majority of people professing to be Christian. I follow that with my response to these tenets as they relate to society in general. I have also included a discussion of sin, which I think needs to be dusted off and explored anew.

This segment is followed by a look at how greed is endemic in our culture, the impact that it is having on our world, and how we as individuals and as the body of Christ are called to turn away from its enticements.

The second part does essentially the same thing regarding the place and role of government within these United States of America. It suggests a continuum of caring that describes a system that exists informally, bringing together church, state, nonprofits, and, in some instances, for-profits to address providing for the common good among the peoples of the

United States. Also included is a short discussion of the economy. The final part provides my side of conversations with you regarding those sticky-wicket issues that currently most often divide us as Christians: abortion, guns, immigration, and homosexuality.

Special Note

Names and circumstances have been changed in the stories included that relate to any clients I worked with to protect their identities. Any similarities between these stories and the experience of others are coincidental.

CHAPTER 1
OF CHURCH

> Never think that you need to protect God. Because anytime you think you need to protect God, you can be sure that you are worshipping an idol.
> —Stanley Hauerwas

> The church must be reminded that it is not the master or the servant of the state, but rather the conscience of the state. It must be the guide and the critic of the state, and never its tool. If the church does not recapture its prophetic zeal, it will become an irrelevant social club without moral or spiritual authority.
> —Martin Luther King Jr.

A House Divided

> Every kingdom divided against itself is laid waste, and no city or house divided against itself will stand.
> —Matthew 12:25b

It has been years since I read C. S. Lewis' *Screwtape Letters*, but I recently had the opportunity to see it as a dramatic presentation. It still has much to say to Christians. If you have not read it, do. If you have, you will recall that it is the story of a demon who has taken on the task of mentoring an apprentice demon. The student has been assigned a Christian to recruit to the other side, and the teacher advises the best ways to break the Christian. We are indeed constantly bombarded by challenges that seem destined to break us apart.

Christians are a house divided—or perhaps even houses divided. Yet we are the followers of one who said, "I ask not only on behalf of these, but also on behalf of those who will believe in me through their word, that they may all be one. As you, Father, are in me and I am in you, may they also be in us, so that the world may believe that you have sent me" (John 17:20–21).

It has been painful to watch what has divided Christians in regards to our government over the past thirty or so years. Highly emotional issues are exacerbated that actually only impact small percentages of the population and are far more complicated than thirty-second sound bites can express. Yet they are pelted at us from every turn. When one starts to wear thin, a new one crops up: abortion, homosexuality, immigration, guns, etc. I am not suggesting that these are issues to be avoided by churches, and I will share some of my thoughts on each later. Here, though, I want to explore how the single-focused nature of these issues is threatening the very purpose, the very heart, of the body of Christ engaged in the world today.

While it may not seem to us that the issues Paul wrestled with are as serious as ours, they were. It mattered a great deal to first-century Christians whether Gentiles needed to be circumcised to be Christians or whether it was all right to eat meat that has been offered to idols. I do believe that had Paul and others not dealt with them, the Christian church would have fallen by the wayside as irrelevant. Is that what we followers of Christ want to happen now?

It might be fun to pick sides regarding athletic teams, wear team colors, show school pride, and sing the alma mater—although I have been known to yell for both Oklahoma State University and Oklahoma University in the same game, and I have no idea what I will do now that Texas Christian University has been moved into the Big 12. Our churches and our government do not exist for sport. There are no red states or blue states in the nation of God. I think it is rather fitting that the primary colors in the church year are purple and green, and neither are what we define as primary colors. Both are colors created from the blending of primary colors.

Chapter ten, verses ten through twelve, of Paul's first letter to the Corinthians might read something like this today: "Now I appeal to you, brothers and sisters, by the name of our Lord Jesus Christ, that all of you should be in agreement and that there should be no divisions among you, but that you should be united in the same mind and the same purpose. What I mean is that each of you says, 'I belong to the conservatives' or 'I belong to the liberals' or 'I belong to the Tea Party' or 'I am one of the 99 percent' or 'I belong to Christ.' Has Christ been divided? Were the conservatives crucified for you? Or were you baptized in the name of the liberals?"

I think the key words here are "united in the same mind and the same purpose." We are fighting over ways and means, not the theology of loving God or loving our neighbors, and I believe that by doing so we are wasting precious resources. We have recently experienced some really serious tornadoes here in Oklahoma that destroyed much property. I heard about the work Catholic charities was doing in providing direct services to those caught in the storm, and later, on the news, I heard the announcement that the Southern Baptists were sending out teams to help people clear their property and salvage whatever they could. Same mind and same purpose, different ways and means—and all are desperately needed as these two groups love God and love their neighbors.

Recently I was chatting with a young woman after my yoga class when she said something to the effect that she could not understand where people who called themselves Christians were coming from. She had been raised in a Christian church, but for her it was like talking about listening to music played on vinyl records—some quaint little cultural history that briefly impacted her life as a child. She is one of those now classified as spiritual, not religious.

The military calls it collateral damage, which includes everything from loss of utilities, to destroyed homes, to the death of innocent children. The military works really hard to avoid collateral damage. When they fail, we hear about it on the nightly news. The church needs to open its eyes and see the collateral-damage consequences of its actions.

My young friend is, I believe, collateral damage. At best, Christians are viewed as hypocrites, preaching love and living animosity, if not outright hate; at worst, we are permanently damaging the lives of people who are lost in the gaps left by our my-way-or-the-highway philosophies. We do not seem to care who gets hurt in the process.

Now I must tell you that I believe with all my heart that God is greater than all our misunderstandings and inabilities to answer God's call to love God and to love our neighbors as ourselves. There is no question in my mind that God will eventually establish a nation of love. That said, we need to consider whether a nation ruled by love is what we really want, because our actions do not seem to indicate that it is. We need to understand that God who created us can turn rocks into bread and will continue with or without us.

Where Is Love?

Where is love? Does it fall from skies above? Is it underneath the willow tree That I've been dreaming of? Where is she? Who I close my eyes to see? Will I

ever know the sweet hello That's only meant for me?
Who can say where she may hide? Must I travel far
and wide? 'Til I am beside the someone who I can
mean something to ... Where ...? Where is love?
—Lionel Bart as sung in the movie *Oliver Twist*[5]

Oliver Twist raises a question that we need to consider. Where is love? Perhaps we might first want to consider this one: What is love? We Americans throw the word around quite loosely, so it may no longer have any more meaning than a bolded exclamation mark. "I just love! chocolate." If God is love, then is God just a bolded exclamation mark? If we consider the question of what love is, we must then also consider what or who God is. I do not intend to write the tome that can even begin to answer that question, nor could I. And I do not want to insult the answer by being flippant in a few paragraphs. So, I ask for some leeway to set forth just a few thoughts on the subject so there is some common ground from which to build our discussion.

God as a creator, by necessity, claims some degree of relationship with the created, and the created have the option to reciprocate. If that link is stressed (or even broken), something about the very beings of both the creator and the created is impacted. The word *create* is by its very nature active and ongoing. Thus, the creator and the created are constantly longing for and entering into a relationship with each other as the created is remolded and remade, hopefully as the old song says: "like thee, divine."[6]

God as a parent is very similar to God as the creator but perhaps with the added quality of the unconditional love of a parent's relationship with his or her child. It might also suggest that the relationship may be with many, between the parent and all of his or her children, allowing love to flow through and among many.

God as the savior takes relationship to another level, not only engaging with the created child but also striving to restore broken links between God and the created child. In so doing, God sets the example for all God's created children to restore broken links between the created child and all of God's other children.

God as a spirit indwells the created child to form an eternal, constant relationship and committed partnership between the creator/parent and the created/children designed to foster the nation of God among all of God's children.

Christians often stop there when defining God, but there is at least one more major category: God as a judge. It seems to me that if love is our purpose, then our love will be the standard by which we are judged. A rereading of Matthew 25 might be appropriate at this point, followed by some intense self-examination. Where is love, indeed?

Paul reminds us what Jesus told us—that Jesus is the judge who ferrets out whether we loved God and loved our neighbors. "For all of us must appear before the judgment seat of Christ, so that each may receive recompense for what has been done in the body, whether good or evil" (2 Corinthians 5:10).

Paul is using words from business to illustrate this concept. He is essentially saying that we must stand before Christ, who will judge what our pay will be for the work we have done. Recompense is pay or reward for services rendered. That is not the image of the final judgment I picked up in childhood, and frankly, I do not like the metaphor related to receiving a paycheck. Maybe that is because I perceive pay as a twenty-first-century concept that is very different from the viewpoint of the first-century Christian. For many, daily pay in the first century meant life. There would be food on the table that day. Whether the family had bread only or also a morsel of meat was determined by how much pay was received—quite different from my middle-class standards of whether I should get the precooked pork loin because I just really do not have time to actually prepare dinner.

There are two very different concepts that I see in Second Corinthians 5:10.

First, Paul is talking about the final judgment at the end of time. For most of us, that will be at some point following our mortal deaths. Paul does not see this as a scary thing or something that ends in eternal damnation as is portrayed in Matthew 25. What he seems to describe is not unlike an exit interview for a retiree. I conducted several of these over my thirty-three-year career in administration. Most of those exit interviews were just downright fun, although pretty emotional, particularly those for people with whom I had worked for many years. For one thing, there were few surprises. When there is a good relationship between a supervisor and supervisee, most mistakes or bad outcomes are opportunities for growth and development occurring in routine, everyday contact. I also tried really hard to recognize jobs well done as they happened. So too might go the exit interview with Jesus.

The exit interviews I remember that were not fun involved people who were leaving with whom I was never able to form a positive relationship. Unlike with Christ, that was probably as much my fault as theirs. We were rarely on the same page at any given time and in a lot of instances my impression was that those individuals wanted to set their own goals and objectives rather than follow the goals and objectives of the agency. For example, I remember well one computer programmer who was constantly creating new applications for our system—I called them bells and whistles, one of the other programmers called it bling-bling. With such bling-bling we could have done amazing things. The only problem was this person would never do the apparently rather boring and mundane but crucial task of adding needed data elements. Thus the data we needed was not available for easy access. This programmer "never had time" to do this basic task. The failure to do assigned work meant others had to do very labor-intensive handwork with raw data. The bells and whistles would have been great had we had the basics first.

What Paul is suggesting, I believe, is that we need to get on the same page with our ultimate judge, Jesus, and follow God's goals to love God and love our neighbors. We are promised the guidance of the Spirit to help discern how, when, and where we are to approach these goals. We do that through constant communication with God through prayer, meditation, Bible study, worship, and other spiritual disciplines. Being a citizen of the nation of God is not a spectator sport. We are called to full participation as God's ambassadors, servants, teachers, etc., while we are in this land.

That leads me to the second concept that I see in this scripture. None of us, not a single one, has been assigned the responsibility of judge in the nation of God. There is only one judge in the nation of God: Jesus Christ. Jesus clearly recognized the need for civil authority, but in the nation of God love always trumps our judgments. We can never know the heart of another person the way God can. Let me say that again: we can never know the heart of another person the way God can.

Do you remember the story of David being anointed king by Samuel? God sent Samuel to the house of Jesse to anoint a new king. Samuel started with the oldest son, who in that culture was the designated next head of the household. But God told Samuel that the oldest, the most obvious choice, was not God's choice. Hear the words from 1 Samuel:

When they came, he looked on Eliab and thought, "Surely the Lord's anointed is now before the Lord." But the Lord said to Samuel, "Do not look on his appearance or on the height of his stature, because I have rejected him; for the Lord does not see as mortals see; they look on the outward appearance, but the Lord looks on the heart." (16:6–7)

We need to trust God to do God's work, Christ to do Christ's work, and the Spirit to do the Spirit's work and set about with all do haste to do our work: loving God and loving our neighbors. Ultimately Christ will make any judgments that matter.

Love does not exist without relationship, and relationship is by its very nature designed to foster more love. In the Hebrew Bible we read that to love is to obey God's command—and God's overarching command is to love.

Jesus talked about mercy and forgiveness and compassion. Paul calls us to recognize God's grace, and surely we are called also to be gracious.

In his book *The Road Less Traveled*, M. Scott Peck defines love as wanting the very best for another. He does not suggest that we decide what is very best for the other! Rather, he opines that love is the will to extend oneself for the purpose of nurturing one's own or another's spiritual growth. Love is as love does. Love is an act of will—both an intention and an action. Will also implies choice. We do not have to love. We choose to love.[7]

As Mother Teresa noted, "I have found the paradox, that if you love until it hurts, there can be no more hurt, only more love."

So, how do we answer Oliver's question? Where *is* love? How do we let an orphan in an institution know God as a creator or parent through our actions? How can we reach the young adult who is already jaded by what she believes are Christian ways? How do we help those who are hungry, naked, or in prison or the stranger that Jesus describes in Matthew 25? How can we tell them, show them, and love them so that they too can know God?

CHAPTER 2
FAITH FED, NOT FEAR BOUND

> Faith is the word that describes the direction our feet start moving when we find that we are loved. Faith is stepping out into the unknown with nothing to guide us but a hand just beyond our grasp.
> —Frederick Buechner, *The Magnificent Defeat*

> But you are a chosen race, a royal priesthood, a holy nation, God's own people [a people for his possession], in order that you may proclaim the mighty acts of him who called you out of darkness into his marvelous light.
> —1 Peter 2:9

Here is one place that I prefer the King James Version, for it uses the phrase "a peculiar people" rather than "God's own people." Today our idea of what is peculiar is not particularly complimentary, but if someone is peculiar, you should be able to identify him or her from the rest of the crowd. I don't think in many instances that is the case regarding Christians in our country today. If it is the case, it may be a negative, not positive, reflection.

Systems theory tells us that the nature of organizations leads them to constantly work toward homeostasis—in other words, a steady state or stability. I do this regularly as I stand on a balance disc, though *wobble* might actually better describe my actions. My goal is to improve my balance. While I am on the balance disc every inch of my body is concentrating on balancing. Gradually I gained the ability to stand on the disc and lift hand weights, but that is about as far as I have gotten. While I only do this a few minutes each day, it has markedly improved my balance in everyday activities.

As Christ's disciples we are called to hone our faith homeostasis to the extent that when we move through the routines of life we are not caught off balance. Our center of being, if you will, needs to be firmly planted in the nation of God rather than in the world at large. If we are not centered in our faith, we are constantly trying to find homeostasis in all the wrong places.

I made likely the hardest decisions I will ever have to make when I was a twenty-two-year-old child welfare worker. Did this child need to be removed from this home to literally save the child's life? Did the need to protect the child outweigh all the damage that removing the child would inevitably cause? Unless you have been in similar situations, you cannot imagine the constant pressure on child welfare staff. Soldiers, police officers, and firefighters know what I am talking about. As a child welfare supervisor, I noted the negative form of reaching for homeostasis. The child welfare job is twofold: protecting children and saving families. Unless one is very firmly ensconced in saving families, the need to protect children became the steady state. Adrenaline was pumping; you could make an immediate impact and move on to the next rush.

The real core of child welfare work, however, is helping families become as whole as possible, if that fails, the goal is helping a child find a home where he or she can thrive. These are poorly supported, multifaceted tasks, involving interaction with all kinds of people, including doctors, psychologists, foster parents, courts, and home aides. It is frustrating and usually involves taking one step forward and two steps back. As a supervisor I tried everything to ameliorate the pressure and battle fatigue but the thing that helped the most was empowering the direct-service workers with the ability to pull away from the situation enough to see the broader picture of why we were doing what we were doing in the first place.

Christians too have a daunting assignment. At times, we, like Joan of Arc, think we have lost our connection with God and try to solve the world's problems on our own. Our linkage with God is strained, and fear of failure, fear of our circumstances, even fear that our belief in God is bogus can all raise their ugly heads.

We are no doubt living in a time of immense change that includes a technological revolution, a communication revolution, and postmodernism rolled into one. I do not anticipate anything slowing down anytime soon. Therefore, we must tenaciously hold on to our source of balance and understand our assignment. We need to love, and through our love and God's empowering love, to let God be God and to be the people God created us to be.

The summer I was sixteen, I worked as a nurse's aide in a nursing home. It was also the summer the Civil Rights Act was being implemented. When I walked into work one morning, I could feel the tension in the air. Staff members were whispering to each other; the supervisors were all business. As I later learned, the evening before, the first black patient had been admitted to the home. At our morning meeting, this new patient was one of the five assigned to me to feed, bathe if needed, etc. When I look back on it now, I think I was chosen for this task on purpose, not because of anything directly related to me, but because the owner knew my mother. I think the head nurse thought that if anybody could handle the situation, it would be Helen Knott's daughter.

Through the course of the morning, as I came to the new patient's room, I gathered my washbasin, soap, washcloth, and towel and stepped across the threshold. I introduced myself and told her—Mrs. Smith, as I will call her—who I was and that I had come to give her a bath. Her body trembled, and she said, "No, you can't." Frankly, I would not want someone walking into my room and trying to give me a bath, so I tried to reassure her, thinking she was concerned about having her privacy so violated. She might have been concerned about her privacy or lack of self-sufficiency, but that was not the problem. She finally said, "You are white. It wouldn't be right."

Wow, I thought, *what do I do about that?* I excused myself and reported the situation to the head nurse, who told me to wait a minute and then left to go talk to the head cook, who was also black and who knew Mrs. Smith. The cook had not been in the room with Mrs. Smith for more than a minute when she came out and told me I could get started. I went in, and this precious soul who had eighty or ninety years of acculturation to the negative allowed me to care for her. Afterward, I asked the cook, "What on earth did you say to her?" The cook said she told Mrs. Smith that I would be fired if Mrs. Smith did not allow me to do my job. This beautiful child of God, Mrs. Smith, sacrificed her fear on the altar of loving me enough to do what she could to save my job.

Fear is like that. It can either make us cowards or give us courage. When we rest our faith in God, God will sustain our courage if we dedicate it to loving God and loving one another.

We cannot and will never legislate our way into the nation of God. As people of God, our vision of such a nation can be reflected in the democracy of which we are a part only when we take the time to enter into dialogue with the other citizens of that democracy and find common ground. We might be truly surprised at what could be accomplished by such an approach. More importantly, I believe that is exactly the task we have signed on for as citizens of the nation of God. Fear not—God is with us.

CHAPTER 3
INCLUSIVE, NOT EXCLUSIVE

> We have learned to say that the good must be extended to all of society before it can be held secure by any one person or any one class. But we have not yet learned to add to that statement, that unless all [people] and all classes contribute to a good, we cannot even be sure that it is worth having.
>
> —Jane Addams

> Civilization is the process in which one gradually increases the number of people included in the term "we" or "us" and at the same time decreases those labeled "you" or "them" until that category has no one left in it.
>
> —Howard Winters

> So God created humankind in his image, in the image of God he created them; male and female he created them.
>
> —Genesis 1:27

Fear is often the parent of exclusion. We fear what we do not know or understand. The very fear of God shares those roots. While some do try to protect themselves from God, we Christians strive to know God more intimately. Is it not the standard set by God for our building relationships with others?

I grew up on a farm in central Oklahoma and went to a tiny rural school. There were seven students in my senior class. The school was consolidated with a nearby school two years after my graduation. I also went to a small rural church. Small communities are microcosms of urban areas. The rich and poor, healthy and sick, honest and dishonest are all there. We were pretty homogenous in my hometown as far as race—mostly white, some American Indians, and for a time one black family with children in our school. In a small community everybody knows everybody else—and probably your parents, siblings, and often your grandparents. I am not suggesting that everything was perfect and everybody loved everybody else, but surprising as it may seem, I did get a good dose of ecumenism—I attended three Bible schools each summer, and everybody in my community participated in the annual Easter pageant—and interacted regularly with people from different socioeconomic backgrounds.

I have now actually lived in cities twice as long as I lived on the farm. To me, the big difference in the interactions between people is that cities tend to group by class and urban churches by class and race—cites are more diverse but much more segregated than rural areas. There is little opportunity for natural interactions among disparate people. It is easy to live in a suburb or even the newly gentrified downtown housing, commute to work, attend church, and even eat in restaurants without ever crossing paths with someone from a different socioeconomic background unless he or she is serving you.

The Mentally Ill

Our country has a terrible system of service for the mentally ill. In my work at the church these past years, addressing the needs of the mentally ill has been one of our greatest, and largely unaddressed, challenges. It certainly makes me wish I had advocated for the mentally ill more when I worked for the government.

While helping to serve a meal at a program for the homeless recently, I sat across from an obviously well-educated woman, somewhat ageless but probably in her early eighties. She had been a music teacher and was now most likely schizophrenic. We had a conversation about our lives. When she heard the name of the church I served, her eyes lit up and she said, "I got married in your church in 1952." She gave me a copy of a song she had written. I promised to put it in our newsletter and did. Our conversation moved in and out of the normal chitchat of two strangers caught up for a moment, touching occasionally on her paranoia of people trying to invade her space and threaten her being.

She is a child of God living on the streets of downtown Oklahoma City, pulling all her belongings in a little cart. She said she had an apartment and was getting teacher's retirement. One of the couples who was also helping that night offered to drive her home. At her request, they dropped her off at the front of an apartment building, watched her enter the front door, and, as they drove away, watched her come out the back door and head down the street, pulling her cart. The demons in her head were apparently less threatening outdoors.

The mentally ill are excluded by our lack of understanding of how to meet their needs and deal with their idiosyncrasies in our ordered world.

People of Diverse Faiths

One of the disadvantages of working at a church, I have discovered, is that I spend most of my time with other Christians. It is really hard to make disciples if everyone with whom one interacts is a disciple. I miss having lunch with a diverse group of people where only a few others and I were the Christians. Some people in my lunch bunch were not religious. Some were Buddhist. One was Muslim.

One of my nonreligious coworkers went to his daughter's day care for a lunch-with-parents event. On his return to work he charged into my office to check out his prayer for the lunch. Apparently he was the only dad who had showed up and the only male present at the luncheon. The director of the day care, assuming that he was active in church, called on him to say grace. If you knew him, you might have made the same mistake. He loves others as he loves himself. He, not wanting to cause a commotion or embarrass his daughter, pulled together something from the prayers he had overheard and wanted me to verify that he had not erred greatly. It was one of the nicest prayers I have ever heard. It made me realize that Fred Craddock was right. There is something to *Overhearing the Gospel*[8], but it cannot happen if we do not interact with the multitudes.

Immigrants

In the months following 9/11, all male legal residents in the United States who were citizens from certain Middle Eastern countries were required to report to immigration and show official papers proving they were here legally. One of the staff members of the division I administered was here on a work visa from one of those countries, and her husband was one of the men who had to respond to this order. They had a four-year-old son at the time who was in his father's care when he went to complete what he thought would be a simple procedure. They had to stand in line for a long time and they met for the first time the gentleman standing behind them in line. My coworker's husband got to the front of the line and, after a computer background check, was notified that he was going to be detained and that his child would be taken into custody. Fearing that he would never get his son back, he quickly turned to his new acquaintance behind him and said to the officials, "My friend will take him to his mother." The stranger did.

My coworker's husband was held for several days without being allowed to see an attorney. A week later, when his case came before the court, it was tossed out. It seems he had the same name as a man who was wanted for smuggling. It was not hard to prove he was not that man. My friend's husband was released.

The arrest happened on the day of our office Christmas party. The year before, we had had such a great time bringing all the staff from our division together with all their families. Beforehand I had discussed the party with my Muslim coworker. I said we could call it a holiday party, but she had no problem with joining in the celebration of Christmas. She offered to bring salmon, and the rest of us spread the word to not put bacon in the green beans or to at least flag it. We had the same plans for 2001. We actually talked about cancelling the party after the husband's arrest but decided the children might not understand. The atmosphere was decidedly different from the year before. As we were putting the food on the table, my coworker walked in with the salmon. She gave her apologies, saying she could not stay. We hugged her. There were tears. And she left. And we thus observed the coming of the Prince of Peace into the world.

There are no borders in the nation of God. While our civil nations may need to establish laws regarding immigration, we Christians need to be mindful of the fact that we are dealing with our brothers and sisters in Christ and ensure that they are treated as we would want any of our own brothers or sisters treated.

-Isms

I do not know what to say about racism, all the bias-based isms as far as that is concerned. One would think that at this point in history, we would be rid of all that hierarchy of exclusion. When will we ever learn that the body of Christ is to include all of God's children and that everyone is God's? Until we understand this simple fact, the fullness of God's love will never flourish across the earth.

When I was in the fifth grade, I spent the night with my best friend. We had recently had two brothers transfer to our school who had been abused and forced to drop out of school at early ages to work. They were placed in foster care with a family in our community. After some basic testing it was determined that the sixteen-year-old, who was probably six feet tall, needed to be in the fifth grade—and that is where he was placed. He was actually behind the rest of us when he started. Because I finished my work quickly, the teacher routinely asked me to help this young man with his reading, which I did.

That evening at my friend's house, we were playing some kind of game on the living room floor and talking about how dumb this big, old guy was. My friend's mother stepped into the doorway coming from the kitchen with a pot in one hand and a dishtowel in the other. She never missed a swipe as she vigorously dried the pot and said, "I want you girls to stop talking about the new student. You aren't any better than anybody else on this earth, and don't you forget it." She turned around and walked back into the kitchen, and just as quickly, she swung back around and with a twinkle in her eye said, "And nobody is better than you." It was a memorable lesson and has stayed with me to this day, and it is my gift from her to you.

CHAPTER 4
EMPATHETIC, NOT JUDGMENTAL

To touch the soul of another human being is to walk on holy ground.

—Stephen Covey

The capacity to give one's attention to a sufferer is a very rare and difficult thing; it is almost a miracle; it is a miracle. Nearly all those who think they have the capacity do not possess it.

—Simone Weil

Judging others makes us blind, whereas love is illuminating. By judging others we blind ourselves to our own evil and to the grace which others are just as entitled to as we are.

—Dietrich Bonhoeffer, *The Cost of Discipleship*

Therefore all things whatsoever ye would that men should do to you, do ye even so to them: for this is the law and the prophets.

—Matthew 7:12

In the mid-1980s, the agency where I worked hired a man who had recently moved here from Chicago to head the division to which I was assigned. Most of the staff had the same first impression: Tom was gay. Most didn't particularly care. The staff did not say anything about it, and neither did he. During his first week, he called each of his unit heads in for a get-to-know-you conversation. He ended the conversation with me by asking if there was anything I did not like about the way things were going regarding my job. There was and I told him. I was the only unit head in the division classified as a programs assistant administrator, which was two pay grades below all the others. The only difference I could see was that I was a woman and all the others were men. He looked surprised, wrote a note, and very graciously said, "I'll look into it." *Sure you will*, I thought as I walked out of his office. He personally delivered to me the papers promoting me to a programs administrator that same week.

It was a year or so later that he started having health problems. I visited him at the hospital, and when he said he had pneumocystis pneumonia, I knew he had full-blown AIDS. People did not live long at that time after a diagnosis of AIDS. It was just a few weeks later that I traveled to Tulsa with him to a meeting of some sort. On the return trip, he got very quiet and finally asked me if I thought homosexuality was a sin. I was very quiet for too long. I did not know what to say. What I finally said was this: "I leave those sorts of things to God. But this I do know: if two people of the same sex loving each other deeply and expressing that love physically was the worst sin on earth, we would be a whole lot closer to the kingdom of God now than we are." I have wondered ever since how Tom took what I said, but that conversation marked the point in my life when I thanked God for assigning Jesus to be the only judge in the nation of God.

It never ceases to amaze me how rich biblical text is. I cannot tell you how many times I have read chapter five of Galatians, because its discussion of the fruits of the spirit is important to me. In a recent reading, I was struck by the last sentence in that scripture, which I highlight here: "By contrast, the fruit of the Spirit is love, joy, peace, patience, kindness, generosity, faithfulness, gentleness, and self-control. *There is no law against such things*" (22–23; emphasis mine). I saw for the first time the infinite breadth of God's judgment and mercy, which is a good guideline for us as we practice our own human judgments.

A Lesson from Dietrich Bonhoeffer

> Judging others makes us blind, whereas love is illuminating. By judging others we blind ourselves to our own evil and to the grace which others are just as entitled to as we are.
>
> —Dietrich Bonhoeffer, *The Cost of Discipleship*

It is a paradox, though a true one, that we cannot fully love another unless we fully love ourselves. This is the wisdom in the scripture that says we are to love our neighbors as we love ourselves. I think because we have fundamental problems with the definition of love and get love all tangled with our own emotions and self-esteem, we never view others as they really are. Our vision of other people is always filtered through our own life experiences and the patterns they draw in our perceptions.

It is also true that we have been enabled fully to love others and ourselves because we have been graced with the love of God, which is not hampered by filters.[9] For some this may be an instantaneous process, but most of us have to acclimate as God's grace gradually clears away the negative patterns etched in our life-experience filters and opens our field of vision so that we can see the image of God in each of God's children.

In the meantime our judgments are cloudy as Bonhoeffer says because "we blind ourselves to our own evil and to the grace which others are just as entitled to as we are." It is as if we know deep in our own hearts that we are unworthy and therefore project what we perceive as our own unworthiness on others, when in God's eyes we are all worthy and growing in humility toward perfection.

People who wear eyeglasses—and most of us do at least wear sunglasses—know what I am talking about. At times some food or dirt flies into our faces and hits right on the lens. These blobs are so big that we cannot miss them, and we must clean our glasses in order to see. Most days, though, it is the accumulation of film that forms from smaller particles that coat both the inside and outside of our glasses and hampers our vision. We will be reading in the evening and realize we are squinting. Taking off our glasses, we hold them to the light and are amazed that we can see anything at all. Our spiritual vision is informed by the light of God, but we must take the time to hold our perceptions up to that light before we see the film on the filter. Further, we must engage with God, whose love is the cleanser that will remove the patterns that have formed and are blocking our sight.

So how does this play out in life? A friend shared with me her struggle with accepting her new daughter-in-law just as she was. Coming from a different socioeconomic class, the daughter-in-law brought markedly different values to the marriage than my friend held. With all good intent to accept her son's wife, my friend tried to help her new relative understand a more enlightened form of homemaking and child rearing than the young woman had experienced in her own life. Indeed, my friend's ways were probably more conducive to healthy living and success in school for the children. They, however, just never seemed to be received until my friend gave up and decided to just enjoy her son and his family as they were. Remarkably, the daughter-in-law started confiding in my friend and seeking her advice on some things that really mattered. Progress is slow but steady as both women carefully maneuver through the minefields of those patterns and as both share a growing relationship with God.

CHAPTER 5
SHARING, NOT HOARDING

Happiness is not so much in having as sharing. We make a living by what we get, but we make a life by what we give.

—Norman MacEwan

The Holy Supper is kept, indeed,
In whatso we share with another's need;
Not what we give, but what we share,
For the gift without the giver is bare;
Who gives himself with his alms feeds three,
Himself, his hungering neighbor, and me.

—James Russell Lowell, from
The Vision of Sir Launfal

When it grew late, his disciples came to him and said, "This is a deserted place, and the hour is now very late; send them away so that they may go into the surrounding country and villages and buy something for themselves to eat." But he answered them, "You give them something to eat."

—Mark 6:35–37

You are the light of the world. A city built on a hill cannot be hidden. No one after lighting a lamp puts it under the bushel basket, but on the lampstand, and it gives light to all in the house. In the same way, let your

light shine before others, so that they may see your
good works and give glory to your Father in heaven.
—Matthew 5:14-16

Now, this may be where you are expecting a lecture on tithing. I actually do practice tithing, giving a tenth of my income in support of the church, believing that there is wisdom in this act as described in the practices of the Hebrew people. Jesus, however, asks for far more than a tenth. It is all or nothing with Jesus. Every breath we take, every thought we have, every task we complete, every resource we possess is to be used toward the glory of God through Jesus Christ our Lord. When we as Christians withhold any of the gifts and talents with which God has gifted us, we are hoarding.

Several years ago I read in the newspaper that an employee of a local hotel in Oklahoma City had been named the national worker of the year for this large chain. It has been awhile, and I may have the facts a bit muddled, but essentially the employee was recognized for this great honor because he did his work to perfection, was always on time and at work when scheduled, was totally dependable, and on top of that was friendly and worked well with his fellow employees and customers. He was responsible for doing the laundry and he was developmentally disabled. He is a shining example of sharing and not hoarding.

I am also a dedicated Oklahoma City Thunder basketball fan. The young team at this writing is also a shining example of those same traits for which the hotel employee was honored at perhaps the opposite end of the income bracket. These players and coaches work hard, hone their skills every day using the talents God has given them, and are very active in community services. Now, I will never be able to shoot like Kevin Durant, run point like Russell Westbrook, or block shots like Serge Ibaka, and you sure would not want me doing your laundry, but I too need to work just as hard at using the talents and skills God has given me, and so do you. In fact I think we may have more opportunity to spread God's love in our daily lives than we do in all our church activities, although a little more love might be helpful at some congregational meetings.

A couple of years ago I participated in a study my regional church was sponsoring based on the book *Witnessing Whiteness*[10] and led by a consultant who is an American Indian. In one of our sessions, this young woman shared something that had recently happened to her and her preschool-age child while standing in line at Wal-Mart. I am paraphrasing from my memory, but essentially she said that the man who was checking out in front of her noticed her and started raving loudly, gesturing in her direction, about how we needed to keep the illegals out of our country.

My first reaction when I heard this story was to think, *Her people where here before his.* Her first reaction was to protect her child, who grabbed her around the legs as he hid behind her in terror. The clerk at the cash register, as if she had not noticed what was going on, asked the man some questions about one of his purchases, making sure she was handling the transaction correctly. With his attention diverted, the man stopped his ranting, answered her questions, paid his bill, and departed. The clerk then apologized to my friend for the previous customer's behavior as she started scanning my friend's purchase. The situation was diffused, and my friend was comforted. Love was delivered as this clerk took action when she did not have to in a way that calmed the situation. She gave of herself to a stranger, a child of God, and she did it in such a way as to not enrage the antagonist further.

Stuff

I have been on a rampage recently to get rid of stuff. I actually am not much of a hoarder. I rarely have problems throwing things away or giving them to others to use. I, however, have lived in the same house for thirty years, and you know you just forget what you have. This all started with not having enough bookshelves for all my books—I guess I do hoard books—and moved to cleaning out drawers and closets. The saddest thing is that I have found things that should have been useful but remained on my shelves well past their expiration dates. I kid you not—I found an almost full can of baking powder with an expiration date of 1977. It was way back in my cabinet. Routinely sharing stuff you no longer need is a great way to be aware of the need to share.

Sharing the Earth

People of the Bible do not need scientists to tell us that we are responsible for the care of the earth. It is right there in the first chapter of the book. Genesis 1:26 says:

Then God said, "Let us make humankind in our image, according to our likeness; and let them have dominion over the fish of the sea, and over the birds of the air, and over the cattle, and over all the wild animals of the earth, and over every creeping thing that creeps upon the earth."

The children of God have all been called to be good stewards of the earth because we have been charged with the responsibility of caring for all the living things on it. I do not think good stewards waste the resources God has provided for us or use it for personal gain at the expense of the other creatures God created. To have dominion means to have absolute ownership. Its very definition implies that we have only ourselves to blame if we mess it up. With absolute ownership we have absolute responsibility, not license.

If plastic, glass, paper, metals, cardboard, and Styrofoam can be used again, does it not just make good stewardship sense to recycle it? And is the same thing not true of buying fuel-efficient vehicles and light bulbs and installing insulation? Further, if God created the earth and all that is in it, God created oil and gas and coal and the wind and the sun, all for our use. God also created us with brains to figure out ways to use these gifts responsibly to maintain the delicate balance of the environment for all who must depend on it for life, including the animals and fish and birds and insects over which God gave us dominion. Here is where we do need the scientists. Denying that there are problems does not make them go away. Helen Keller may have said it best: "Science may have found a cure for most evils; but it has found no remedy for the worst of them all—the apathy of human beings."[11]

Responsible Investing

Do you know what companies are included in your retirement plan, mutual funds, IRAs, and 401(k)s? If you own stock in a company, do you look at anything but the bottom line? We may all be trying to live within our means, support the church and other charities, and be good stewards of the earth while living or planning to live off income that has not been earned ethically or even wisely. Just as it is each of our duty to know what is going on with our government and elected officials, it is also important that we be active and engaged stakeholders in our investments. We have every right to hold to the fire the feet of those who are charged with growing our investments. They are being paid very well to do their jobs. It seems we human beings need a depression or a near depression to make us open our eyes and see how the financial world is working. As long as the earnings are good, it is easy to not see risky behaviors.

Intentionality

Paul talks about being perfect. Now, none of us is perfect, and initially, my reaction is to think that it was pretty audacious of him to even suggest such a thing. He further talks about reaching for the goal like a well-trained athlete. Those folks never quit. But really is, that any different from challenging us to be Christlike? To be the children of a God who is love? In the final analysis, we must cling to the faith that we are never alone in our quest—but we are indeed called to a quest. We are a part of that wonderful body of Christ, so none of us has to do everything or anything by ourselves. The Spirit is with us, ready and willing to run whatever race we have been called to run from the moment we take our first steps on the track.

To do this we must practice the art of intentionality, living our lives under the rule of love. That requires us to continuously challenge our actions and reactions to ensure that they are passing what I call the test of love. Does what I am pursuing past the test of love? Is it of God?

I believe that God created each of us with special talents and skills but spreads before us more choices than we can imagine regarding how to use those to God's glory. One of my passions is to ensure that every able person in the world has access to a means of earning a living wage and is enabled to take advantage of that access. The singularity of that passion broadens my palate of interest to child care, education, teen pregnancy, rehabilitation and more. I can pursue that passion as close to home as supporting adult education and working on tax legislation or as far away as impacting world trade by always looking for fair-trade-certified products. While my buying fair trade coffee may not seem like much, the whole body of Christ buying fair trade coffee makes a difference. We must never forget the synergy that comes from functioning within the body of Christ. Remember, "For where two or three are gathered in my name, I am there among them" (Matthew 18:20).

The real challenge is to check our thoughts and actions against that test of love. Each morning take a few minutes to set goals for the day to help you live your love of God and love of your neighbor, and each evening, evaluate how well you did. Examine whether it is more important to you to get your way or God's. Finally, be in silence with God for a time and let God give you feedback. Jesus routinely withdrew to be with God from the very beginning when he went into the wilderness to face his own demons to the garden of Gethsemane. We need to let God reflect back on us what we may not be able to see in ourselves.

This might be as good a place as any to explore sin. What is it? What is its relevance in our modern society?

CHAPTER 6
SIN

I think sin for many Christians is an arcane word that has little meaning today. For other Christians, sin is all about obeying rules or not obeying them. Sound familiar? Jesus was indeed a prophet for our times when he told the parable of what we call the prodigal son.[12] It is hard for many Christians born in the United States to consider that both sons in this story were lost: one by wasting his life, the other by wasting his father's love. So what is sin all about, anyway?

The best way I can get my mind around sin as Christians view it is to describe sin in modern nomenclature as being out of sync with God. Once by accident a televised Thunder basketball game began its broadcast using the Spanish-language radio station's play calling. Now, I have actually studied Spanish, but I certainly do not have the capability of following a fast-paced basketball game called in Spanish. I tried muting the sound, and I enjoyed watching, but I did not understand everything that was happening. I tuned into the local radio broadcast of the game and received reporting I could understand, but the radio was about fifteen seconds ahead of the action on TV. I heard someone was going to make a basket, and then I watched them make it. Not fun.

Being out of sync with God is like that. To sin is to totally mute God out of our lives, like the younger brother in the prodigal son story. We do this perhaps because we truly do not understand the language that is being spoken to us—or we understand it but do not like what is being said. The other response happens when we "forget" that we are in a partnership with God and that God has the lead—when we run ahead of or behind God's will for us.

It is important to note in the parable of the prodigal son that the story never says that the older son was doing wrong by taking care of business; his sin was in his inability to accept that his father could love both his totally irresponsible brother and him in the same way. In the older brother's context, love is something one has to earn; the harder you work, the more love you get. He was working for brownie points, not for the sake of furthering his father's kingdom. God's love for each of his children is independent of God's love for each of the others.

This description of our relationship with God has not changed since the garden of Eden, where we learned through our predecessors that God gave us the option to stay in sync with God, with the understanding that the more we move away from God, the less likely we are to benefit from God's abiding presence.

Based on our Hebrew background, sin at its foundation has the connotation of missing the mark or going astray from God.[13] The Israelites viewed God's will as being revealed in the laws established to provide both order to society and fidelity to God. The law gave shape and practical guidance in not missing the mark and in staying on the right path. A simplistic example of this is our traffic laws. Stop signs and speed limit rules are all designed to keep traffic moving in a safe and progressive manner. Obeying traffic laws is not our goal. They are aids to helping us reach our desired destination safely.

There are 613 laws in the Torah. These range from "you shall have no other gods before me" (Exodus 20:3) to "you shall not wear clothes made of wool and linen woven together" (Deuteronomy 22:11). Many of these laws seem outdated to us today but may indeed have been meaningful for that time and place regarding a relationship with God, civil law, health, safety, and even etiquette. I am struck that some still have great merit among many people in that they often apply more to others, not to themselves.

The challenge today is to ferret out the basis of such laws as guidance for not going astray from God in a world where we wear few clothes that are not blends of some kind or other. Indeed, our culture now identifies some sexual behaviors as going astray, at least from social norms, that the ancient Hebrews practiced with impunity—polygamy, for example. Just because there were no laws against it does not mean we should practice it now. Women in most instances are no longer seen as incubators, probably primarily because the birth of many children is no longer necessary for the economic stability of the tribe. Similarly, laws like Leviticus 18:22[14] and 20:13[15] may have had more to do with the lack of offspring from the nature of such relationships than anything else. Nowhere does the law address sex acts between two women. It seems the ancients believed that semen contained the "seed" of humanity and that the womb was the fertile "soil" in which it was planted.

Whether for practical reasons or spiritual ones, all societies trend toward established norms. Anything that goes against norms may be considered an outlier. This can result in such things being identified as sacred symbols, such as a white buffalo, or condemned, such as left-handedness. Of course, there are those who do not believe in God and explain all life through the phases and stages of societal development. The thoughtful worship of God, however, calls us believers to examine our norms as they are set forth in laws or rules, whether formal or informal, against what we know about God to ascertain what is in sync with God and what is not—what hits the mark and does not stray from the path. We know that God's basic rules for life are to love God and to love our neighbors as we love ourselves, and these laws of love are always the litmus test against which we must weigh all our norms.

I was privileged to attend a seminar at which Pamela Eisenbaum[16] spoke about the dynamic nature of the law in Judaism. My understanding of what she noted was that the Jewish faith has a long tradition of reviewing the laws of Moses, not to question them, but to assure that they remain relevant to practicing Jews in their time and place. She gave an example of the need to deal with the invention and use of the electric light bulb and decide whether the flipping of the light switch would constitute work on the Sabbath. While this may seem mundane to us today, it goes to the heart of the proper observance of the Sabbath that includes not working. Lighting fires was work. When the laws were originally written, the production of artificial light was related to work, not the availability of light.

Jesus perhaps was carrying forward this tradition of reviewing the laws when he responded to those who criticized his disciples for plucking heads of grain in a cornfield on the Sabbath. Jesus said, "The sabbath was made for humankind, and not humankind for the Sabbath" (Mark 2:27). He was not questioning the importance of observing the Sabbath but exploring in more depth what makes the Sabbath important and holy. In a world where one sits while working or watching TV or reading, a good brisk walk away from distractions might be more conducive to making the Sabbath holy today.

We talked earlier about considering the laws of love. Living within these laws of love is God's ultimate purpose for us. Within Judaism, the coming of the Messiah is the point at which sin will be set aside and sinlessness established in the messianic kingdom.[17] As people who acknowledge Jesus as the Messiah, we Christians are called to live out our lives every day, loving God and loving our neighbors as ourselves and being a conduit for God's love to spread from our homes to the ends of the earth. Through the grace of God in the life, death, and resurrection of God's son, Jesus, we believe the messianic nation has been initiated.

What did Jesus tell us and, probably more importantly, show us about sin? First, we need to acknowledge that Jesus was often castigated by some religious leaders of the time regarding what they perceived as Jesus' sins: plucking and eating grain on the Sabbath, healing on the Sabbath, and associating with misfits. Jesus was never heavy into castigating anyone about his or her sins. In general, when people came to Jesus, he accepted them just as they were, and rather than demanding a confession of sin, Jesus generally asked people, "What do you need?" or "What do you want?"

Jesus understood that he was the way to the end of sin. He had come to reconcile all people to God. We have been called to introduce all people to Jesus Christ, just as they are, and if any reconciliation is needed to let Jesus do it. He is certainly better equipped to do that than any of us are. If we know he can meet our needs and alleviate the pressure to go astray, we must know that he can do it for others. After all, he knows exactly where each of us stands in our loving God and loving our neighbors as we love ourselves. No one else knows that. That does not mean we are to convert and desert those people who pass our way. We are called to the extraordinary task of loving them for who they are and who they are becoming as a continuation of our becoming like Christ.

One of my favorite scriptures is Matthew 11:28–30:

> Come to me, all you that are weary and are carrying heavy burdens, and I will give you rest. Take my yoke

upon you, and learn from me; for I am gentle and humble in heart, and you will find rest for your souls. For my yoke is easy, and my burden is light.

You who were not raised on a farm may not get this. Frankly, I have only seen oxen work at fairs and pulling contests. Their working in the field was before my time. There is synergy in two animals pulling together, so a yoke is placed around their necks, and together their power becomes greater than each of them pulling separately. The trick is that one of the animals has to set the pace, and the other must keep up, or havoc occurs. When we are yoked with Jesus, we cannot either drag our feet or try to beat him to the end of the row.

Our friend Paul was zealous for the Lord. According to him, he never broke any of the laws and studied under the most admired teachers. When those rabble-rousing people came along claiming that Jesus was the Messiah, Paul (then called Saul) set about with all due haste to shut them down before they ever got started. He was pulling hard against God's yoke. Now Christ surely saw the potential in Paul, but this guy was so far out of step that he needed some personal attention—and that is what he got on the road to Damascus. While we have many dramatic stories throughout Christian history, we all need such direct intervention at times, whether it is a moment of inspiration while reading scripture or the gentle nudging of a fellow Christian. Paul was so stunned he took a few years to study Hebrew scripture, trying to make sense of what happened. Apparently he did, and we have been graced with his gleanings ever since. While Paul understood that he was to love God, he was brought to his knees by gaining the understanding that God loved and valued him.

A lot of our divisions would be healed if each of us could fully grasp that amazing, wonderful fact. Because once we accept God's love, we can trust that God has our backs and the backs of all God's other children. We just need to love God and love all his other children too.

As Paul ventured through the Gentile world, he had to deal over and over again with Mosaic law and with the Messiah's taking away the sins of the world. When he was in his self-exile to study, he probably came upon Jeremiah 4:4: "Circumcise yourselves to the Lord, remove the foreskin of your hearts, O people of Judah and inhabitants of Jerusalem, or else my wrath will go forth like fire, and burn with no one to quench it, because of the evil of your doings." And he probably also found Joel 2:13: "Rend your hearts and not your clothing. Return to the Lord, your God, for he is gracious and merciful, slow to anger, and abounding in steadfast love, and relents from punishing." When he reviewed them that time, he would have read then with the new perspective of a follower of the promised one, the Messiah. Paul may also have heard the words of Stephan echoing from the earth where Stephan was stoned at Paul's feet: "You stiff-necked people, uncircumcised in heart and ears, you are forever opposing the Holy Spirit, just as your ancestors used to do" (Acts 7:51).

Later in Paul's ministry, when he returned to Jerusalem to discuss how to approach the different cultures within which he was now working, he came prepared for a great debate, and apparently it transpired. It was not Paul who had the last word, however; it was Peter, the one who loved Jesus but denied him. Even so, Jesus commissioned Peter to build his church. He took a giant step in doing that by enabling Paul's ministry. Peter's words were not to be taken lightly.

> My brothers, you know that in the early days God
> made a choice among you, that I should be the one

through whom the Gentiles would hear the message of the good news and become believers. And God, who knows the human heart, testified to them by giving them the Holy Spirit, just as he did to us; and in cleansing their hearts by faith he has made no distinction between them and us. Now therefore why are you putting God to the test by placing on the neck of the disciples a yoke that neither our ancestors nor we have been able to bear? On the contrary, we believe that we will be saved through the grace of the Lord Jesus, just as they will. (Acts 15:7–11)

Now, most of us do not think about circumcision as anything other than a medical issue. But Peter's statement—particularly the part about placing a yoke on the neck of the disciples that neither we nor our ancestors have been able to bear—has relevance for us today in our discussions about such things as homosexuality. We are asking that homosexuals not just avoid adultery and promiscuity but give up their sexuality. Is that something heterosexuals are willing to bear even if we could?

Paul was much more assertive about the issue of circumcision in Galatians 5:2–6:

Listen! I, Paul, am telling you that if you let yourselves be circumcised, Christ will be of no benefit to you. Once again I testify to every man who lets himself be circumcised that he is obliged to obey the entire law. You who want to be justified by the law have cut yourselves off from Christ; you have fallen away from grace. For through the Spirit, by faith, we eagerly wait for the hope of righteousness. For in Christ Jesus neither circumcision nor uncircumcision counts for anything; the only thing that counts is faith working through love.

Isn't it ironic that while we are commissioned to do two very proactive actions against which there are no laws, loving God and loving our neighbors as ourselves, we spend most of our energy trying to obey laws, rules, and norms or making other people obey our laws, rules, and norms? When all learn to love God fully and to love our neighbors as ourselves, there will be no need for the thou-shalt-nots. We Christians are charged with the responsibility of living and spreading that good news.

Many Christians hold precious 1 Corinthians 13, a description of love. The question is, do we live it? I will join you in a challenge to read that chapter and to experiment with living it for six weeks. I have heard it takes six weeks of practice to make something a habit. Let us try it and see how it impacts our lives.

Though we have received God's grace, we still find ourselves caught up in sin. We must open ourselves to the healing love of God and submit our times of being out of sync regularly as a part of our growth in discipleship. I fear, though, that we have so adapted to some forms of sin that their practice has become our norm. The Hebrew Bible is full of such stories, and the primary culprit is idolatry, worshipping things or people rather than God. We do not bow down before statues of Baal or other effigies, and we do not use the word *idol* very much anymore unless we are describing a rock singer or actor or TV show. Yet they still stand in the way of our becoming the people of God as God would have it to be. One of the most insidious forms of idolatry is greed, and I think we need to take a closer look at it.

Greed

> It has always seemed strange to me... the things we admire in men, kindness and generosity, openness, honesty, understanding and feeling, are the concomitants of failure in our system. And those traits we detest, sharpness, greed, acquisitiveness, meanness, egotism and self-interest, are the traits of success. And while men admire the quality of the first they love the produce of the second.
> —John Steinbeck

> An intriguing paradox of the 1990s is that it isn't called a decade of greed.
> —Paul Samuelson

> For you were called to freedom, brothers and sisters; only do not use your freedom as an opportunity for self-indulgence, but through love become slaves to one another. For the whole law is summed up in a single commandment, 'You shall love your neighbour as yourself.' If, however, you bite and devour one another, take care that you are not consumed by one another.
> —Galatians 5:13–15

Now what I have said up to this point is all well and good, but it does not mean a thing in the world in which we find ourselves. Because faith convictions, values, and character, have little to do with what actually occurs in the macro system known as the United States and more and more in each states. This country is suffering from an epidemic of greed that, if not checked, will be its undoing. I fear we all have a touch of the greed. This is nothing new. The prophets railed against it. Jesus certainly addressed it head-on. Yet greed is so stealthy that we probably never realized when it hit us.

What is greed? I think greed actually grows from the very neutral word *gain*. Gain is essential in all aspects of life. We strive to gain knowledge, wisdom, and a better life for our families and our neighbors. We have certainly seen the downside of inertia—life with no gain—and even the backward movement of loss. Our recent economic failures threaten us with the possibility that our children and our children's children will not have the abundant life we have known, if indeed what we experienced or are experiencing is an abundant life. Jesus perhaps said it best in Luke 9:25: "What does it profit them if they gain the whole world, but lose or forfeit themselves?" Here we draw closer to the meaning of greed. Greed is a step across the line from healthy gain to grasping, selfish desire for something that at the moment is more important than anything else. This type of gain does not care who might get hurt or who might get left out. At its worst, there is no love of neighbor in greed. Colossians 3:5 defines greed as idolatry in a list of things we are to put to death.

Each time we hold something in higher esteem than God, our relationship with God is damaged. Jesus clearly wanted us to experience God fully and completely so that we could fully experience being the people God created us to be. John 10:7–15 addresses this well:

> So again Jesus said to them, "Very truly, I tell you, I am the gate for the sheep. All who came before me are thieves and bandits; but the sheep did not listen to them. I am the gate. Whoever enters by me will be saved, and will come in and go out and find pasture. The thief comes only to steal and kill and destroy. I came that they may have life, and have it abundantly.

> "I am the good shepherd. The good shepherd lays down his life for the sheep. The hired hand, who is not the shepherd and does not own the sheep, sees the wolf coming and leaves the sheep and runs away—and the wolf snatches them and scatters them. The hired hand runs away because a hired hand does not care for the sheep. I am the good shepherd. I know my own and my own know me, just as the Father knows me and I know the Father. And I lay down my life for the sheep."

When more than one person gets caught up in greed, it festers and becomes systemic, impacting not only our ability to love God but also our ability to love our neighbors as we love ourselves.

One of the best ways to avoid dealing with our united greed is to constantly keep ourselves distracted by what we perceive as other major problems that impact the moral fabric of our country. Thus, when our governmental representatives start to mess around with legislation that might attempt to bring our wall of greed down, someone with a hidden agenda cries, "Abortion!" or "Homosexual!" or "Illegals!" or "Guns!" At that point, the subject is quickly refocused onto these "acceptable" moral fabric issues. Don't believe me? Think about how much time our federal and state senators and representatives spent on these four issues over the past several years. Count how many bills were considered related to these subjects. Not counting public appearances to point out the error of the other party's ideas, how much time has been taken resulting in constructive action to address the major economic and job-related problems faced by the United States over the past several years? *Gridlock* has become the word to describe government today. We must have the looming threat of shutting down the government to get essential bills passed.

I wrote this with the 2012 election campaign in the background. It is appalling how much money was spent on those campaigns. Even more critical is the amount of money or other considerations that are provided by lobbyists to control legislation.

We the people are the only ones who can stop this circus, but we first must deal with the greed we cannot see in our own lives. Our elected representatives are giving us exactly what we seem to want.

I think a friend of mind said it best: "I'm tired of paying all these taxes." I replied,

"But we need to continue to have roads built, etc.,"

And she said, "The government is supposed to pay for those things."

If greed has so infiltrated our way of life, what is the cause? I believe it is fear. I am one of the older baby boomers, and some say we are so "different" because of the introduction of nuclear power with the dropping of the atom bombs that ended World War II. I certainly remember the air raid drills, where we sat under our desks with our heads down, covering them with our arms. I also remember having dreams about Russians coming to get me. My Russians looked a lot like the Transformers with which our children play today. The theory was that we were made aware of how finite we actually are and thus developed the curse of instant gratification. I am not sure it was just the nuclear age, but progress in general leaves us breathless. We are afraid that the world is going too fast and that we cannot keep up with it. We are afraid of that which is strange to us, and more and more of the world is strange to us as it gets smaller and smaller. We are afraid of the stranger.

Does this sound to you like the Israelites following the death of David and the division of that country? Israel did not remain united following its civil war. It eventually found itself surrounded by hungry, rising world powers. Turning a blind eye to the reality that surrounded them, its citizens partied hearty, forgetting the God who created them, failing to love one another, and ignoring their call to be a blessing to other nations. They practiced their religion but not their faith and ended up slaves in Babylon.

Now, I do not think that God wants any of God's children to fall like the Israelites did. God did not what them to fail, but to be what God had created them to be: a people who could be a blessing to all nations and serve as midwives to the birthing of the nation of God. God will be with any and all people who understand God's purpose and work with all their hearts, minds, souls, and strength to make God's nation a reality today. For that to happen, we must do our jobs of loving and trust that God, who is greater than all of us together, is working God's will among us through our love.

Most Christians know that Acts 2 tells the story of the coming of the Holy Spirit. Some know that Acts 1:1–11 tells the story of the ascension of Jesus Christ. Verses twelve through twenty-six are not so memorable. I, however, had one of those aha moments recently while reading the second half of Acts 1. It is a rather mundane report, like listening to the reading of board minutes. It tells of the disciples deciding they needed to replace Judas. This was predicated on their need to move on toward the purposes that Jesus had left with them. Jesus had identified twelve leaders, and so they thought returning to twelve leaders would be a good starting point, I guess. It is all rather matter-of-fact. They identified appropriate candidates and then had them draw stones from a container. The one who got the special stone replaced Judas. His name was Mathias.

He rather represents all of the rest of us, I think, but that was not my aha experience. This action, this naming of Mathias, was the first indication that the disciples had processed their grief and were ready to go to work. And next, in Acts 2, we see the tongues of fire and rushing wind. I think God was saying, "It's about time. Let's go. I'm with you." Rather than run away from our God-given task of loving God and loving our neighbors and quaking behind locked doors or partying like there's no tomorrow, it is time for us to get to work. Trust God. Like in Acts 2, God is telling us, "It's about time. Let's go. I'm with you."

I don't even pretend to understand our global economy or the intricacies of diplomacy or the science of global warming. I do have some rather strong opinions about the ultimate goals for those areas that might be a good place to start. I probably know too much about welfare, health care, etc., and, yes, I have strong opinions about those also. Many of us do, but it is time we come to the table, the most fitting place for Christians, and allow love to course through our differences.

So how does a citizen of the nation of God coalesce with being a citizen of the United States of America?

CHAPTER 7
OF STATE

If the purpose of Christians is to love God and to love our neighbors as ourselves, what is the purpose of government? Government exists to assure the common good—from local issues that tend to be more specific, to global issues that tend to be more general. Thus the city may set rules about traffic, assessing fines to assure compliance. It provides for the police, who enforce those rules so that commercial and personal transportation may proceed in an orderly, effective, and efficient fashion. The federal government establishes laws to ensure that interstate and international transportation do the same. All levels of government must work with each other and with all other entities who may be involved with transportation. This is an easy example. The assurance of the common good, however, is involved in every aspect of our lives, although all may not be as clear-cut as transportation—though it too has its moments of controversy. Remember the bridge to nowhere? I do not like labels, as I think they carry more weight than they should, but there exist differences of opinion among individuals and groups regarding how involved government should be in providing for the common good and in defining what issues are relevant to the common good.

There is also a difference of opinion regarding whether governments should be proactive or reactive to situations—or, rather, where the balance of resource use can best be found between the two. It is always more cost-effective to be proactive,

I believe, but that requires special attention regarding the point where being proactive loses its cost-effectiveness. Insurance is a good example of this. Many homeowners choose not to carry flood insurance if their home is not in a flood-prone area on the gamble that during their stay in the home one of those hundred-year floods will not occur. The federal government has in place a system to be reactive with low-interest loans and other disaster relief for such a devastating event in its role of addressing the common good. Along with state governments, it is proactive in identifying flood-prone areas so that homeowners can make good decision about insurance. Similar programs exist to react to farm crises when droughts or other situations threaten crops and thus threaten the food supply.

Governments tend to be more proactive in relation to such things as national defense and health. We keep a strong group of well-trained military personnel and the entire supporting infrastructure to be ready, if needed, in the great hope that they will never be needed. Since we have been at war for so long, we probably do not see this as a proactive part of government, but hopefully, over the next few years, as the war in Afghanistan ends, we will return to having a ready defense and searching for that fine balance of what is enough but not too much. Local governments face this challenge all the time in regard to police and fire safety. I think we all would prefer to have both of these entities function on the proactive side.

I have often wondered how much better off the United States would be had we dealt with health care back in the 1970s when President Jimmy Carter tried to address it. The problems were actually more manageable at that time than they are now. Hillary Clinton was charged with leading a group to find answers to providing affordable health care in the early 1990s. While much work was done, nothing resulted. We the people demanded the right to have our cake and eat it too, and now we are paying and will continue to pay a high price for our greed while allowing the health care problem to fester near the point of no return.

In a democracy, education is probably the most essential proactive activity. Democracies are dependent on a knowledgeable citizenry.

According to the US Constitution, our federal government's purpose is to:

- form a more perfect union,
- establish justice,
- ensure domestic tranquility,
- provide for the common defense,
- promote the general welfare, and
- secure the blessings of liberty to ourselves and our posterity.

The first thing I note about this list is that our purpose as a nation is living, active, and engaged, not set in stone. Our founders foresaw that we would no doubt face many issues that they could not even imagine, so they set forth basic tenets toward which we are always to strive. For example, our purpose clearly recognizes our interdependence within these United States yet lays the groundwork for the development of our interdependence as one nation in a world of many nations.

I am also struck that the first purpose listed—to form a more perfect union—sounds a whole lot like Jesus' desire that we all be one. I fear as the church goes, so goes our nation, often ignoring this call for solidarity to our own peril. It literally took years to write the US Constitution. Our founders knew, better than anyone, how noisy democracy can be, and yet their intent to maintain it was etched deeply in the first purpose mentioned. Seventy or so years later, we would render the ultimate challenge to such a union through a bloody Civil War. The union, though scarred, still stands.

When I look at these purposes as a whole, the picture I see being drawn is the protection of the "common good," but that is indeed a hard concept to wrap one's head around. It has a quality of interdependence from which we Americans may shy away. While we value individualism greatly, we might do well to heed Benjamin Franklin's observation at the signing of the Declaration of Independence: "We must all hang together, or assuredly we shall all hang separately."

It is possible to define areas of common good that do not relate to our faith but merely our self-preservation. Health codes and their enforcement have done much over the past centuries to curb the relentless deaths of loved ones from dysentery or small pox or the plague. Even if we do not care a bit about our neighbor, we certainly care about what they might be spreading. I track eight lines in my genealogy work, and I do not have a single line that did not have several deaths from what we would describe today as common childhood diseases until the first quarter of the twentieth century. In 2012, West Nile Virus reared its ugly head again, and I read in the paper that the increase can possibly be tracked to cuts in funding of programs to reduce the incidence of disease-carrying mosquitoes[18].

Many argued regarding the Affordable Health Care Act that they should not be made to buy insurance, while health care providers are saying that the cost of the uninsured is being passed on to the insured. The health care providers cannot stay in business if their actual cost is not being covered.

I suppose an alternative solution to making people pay insurance would be repealing all our Good Samaritan laws and encouraging the health care industry to just turn all away who could not pay for their care, risking at least contagion and at worst anarchy. Or we could go to a one-payer system where all are covered through a governmental program. I personally would not want to go to a health care provider who could turn away someone in need of care, and I do not know of any that could. I would be satisfied with a one-payer system, but the compromise that was reached was to regulate the requirement that all who meet certain income standards help pay for the cost of their own health care. This solution meets the common good test and is probably truer to our economic system than a one-payer system. Do you see the dilemma of finding the common good?

Those of us who claim to be people of faith have an even higher standard to meet: How can our love of God and love of our neighbors be expressed in our government's attempts to address the common good? And perhaps just as importantly, how can we address the difference between our standards and governmental responses?

Let us look at the components of our federal government's purposes in light of the common good and God's good.

CHAPTER 8
PROMOTE THE GENERAL WELFARE

While general welfare is not listed first, it probably has a great deal of overlap with the church, and it is a subject with which I am very familiar. So I will start there. When I Googled the phrase "general welfare," I got listing after listing of people or groups trying to explain that our founders, when they wrote this, were not talking about welfare. Isn't that interesting? I first learned that *welfare* was a dirty word in the United States in the 1970s, when the agency for which I worked felt compelled to change its name from the Department of Public Welfare to the Department of Institutions, Social and Rehabilitative Services. Try writing that on a line labeled *Employer*. This was during the transition from the Great Society to an emphasis on fraud, waste, and abuse.

I think when our founders wrote "general welfare" they meant "general welfare." Small pox was epidemic in the colonies. Breadwinners were called away from home to fight, leaving mothers and children to fend for themselves. As the nation developed, sanitation systems were needed, transportation issues had to be addressed, and organized means of dealing with fires and other disasters had to be created. The government serves the common good in regard to the well-being of its people as a whole when singular or limited situations are not allowed to become major threats to society. Just as a military force is necessary to ensure the common defense, systems must be present to ensure the general welfare.

We want the Centers for Disease Control to be actively engaged in health safety. We want people to be immunized. And, if for no other reason than our own well-being, we do not want people dying in the streets from starvation or illness. Government is the only entity with the broad-brush authority and resources to deal effectively with such issues.

The important word here is *general*, and the challenge is to maintain a healthy balance among federal, state, and local governments while coordinating with a broad array of nongovernmental organizations and perhaps individuals to address more specific situations.

Continuum of Caring

There exists an informal continuum of caring in the United States—throughout the world, actually—that needs to be recognized and fostered. On one end is the highly structured, international, justice-driven responses to ensure the common good, and at the other end is the unstructured, one-on-one, mercy-driven responses. In between is a hodgepodge of mercy and justice that has developed through the years to fill identified gaps and, when needed, to hold the other participants in the continuum of caring to a higher standard.[19]

Government tends to skew toward the highly structured, international/intergovernmental, generally oriented, justice-driven responses. Faith-based individuals and groups tend to skew toward the unstructured, one-on-one, specifically oriented, mercy-driven responses. Both, however, are represented on either end of the continuum. For example, the pastor who visits a person in the hospital represents the mercy end; the government paying the Medicare charges represents the justice end. There is a bit of mercy and a bit of justice in both actions. On the other hand, the governor who pardons a prisoner is showing mercy, albeit perhaps based on a justice issue. The first responders to disasters in some countries are often people from nongovernmental organizations because they are already there serving other needs. When Haiti was so devastated a few years ago, nongovernmental organizations were already meeting some basic needs when the much-needed military hospital ships arrived to address the greater volume of care needed. Again, there is a bit of justice and a bit of mercy in both actions.

Addressing the magnitude of major issues in the United States and around the world requires an organic response that includes structured and unstructured work, is local and global, and results in mercy and justice.

I worked with a family once in which both parents were developmentally disabled. They were good people. He worked hard and adequately supported the family. They had a ten-year-old son who was a great kid, doing well in school but not getting the stimulation he really needed at home. As a representative of the government, I had nothing to offer this family. They did not qualify for or need public assistance of any kind, and they were nurturing and caring parents. One of our local churches had a group that wanted to offer their time and talent. So I asked them to refer this family to a volunteer. After a church family was identified, the family with the ten-year-old was asked if they would like to meet new friends, and they were willing. A woman from that church group became their friend. She and her family started inviting the son to participate in activities with them, introducing the son to a broader world while respecting and honoring his parents for the wonderful people that they were. The church group would never have known this family with the ten-year-old existed had they not contacted our office and said, "What can we do to help?"

I underwent a major transition when attending a meeting at my church while I worked for the government. For one thing, at work, I dealt with planning that resulted in the spending of millions of dollars with a total budget in the billions impacting almost every citizen of the state in one way or another. These services were based on laws and regulations that had already been defined and long-term goals set with limited leeway for innovation. At the church, even at the regional one, we generally started from scratch with limited resources or a need to raise resources for some identified need that was often more global than specific. I had to learn the gift of the spirit of patience in these meetings and sometimes preferred the King James Version's description of this fruit of the spirit as "longsuffering." The church addressing the problem of hunger, for example, was hard for me to consider when hundreds of thousands of Oklahomans were considered food insufficient. But the sustenance provided by local food banks immediately addresses the hunger of those who do not qualify for governmental assistance or families whose supply of food runs out before the month ends.

From working with individuals like the volunteer just described to contracting for services, I had been working from a government perspective with what we now call faith-based groups for twenty years before this name came into vogue. My experience was that the faith-based groups understood the separation of church and state and followed the rules religiously, as is their normal practice. For example, we licensed all child care facilities, but if a child care facility wanted to receive government-sponsored child care subsidies, it had to sign an agreement that it would not discriminate based on race. In all honesty, we had a few back in the early part of my career that chose not to sign the document and thus could not receive subsidy payments. They could still be licensed. We were able to pay child care subsidy payments to churches that did sign the agreement because we allowed parents to choose in which facility they placed their children.

Some of the best drug and alcohol treatment programs in the country, particularly for people on the street, are operated by religious groups. We contracted for these services, again encouraging our clients to get drug and alcohol treatment, but allowing them to select the provider. And faith-based groups have been providing for the adoption and fostering of children since long before the United States was a twinkle in anyone's eye. We tried not to interfere with the nongovernmental activities of these organizations and groups, and they were always frank and straightforward when any of our requirements was not something they could support. In most of these arrangements, money did not cross hands unless it was paying for something like child care that was being paid to the private sector as well. It is not hard to state, in writing if necessary, where any lines might need to be drawn to assure that separation of church and state is maintained. There is also a plethora of private nonprofits, which may or may not have religious affiliations and work well with governmental agencies that provide for the needs of citizens.

Paul describes our being the body of Christ in Romans 12 and First Corinthians 12, explaining that we are all called to be a part of one body, each of us doing his or her own part. As you read the previous pages in this book, it is easy to see the areas in which I have some preparation, knowledge, and experience and the areas in which I do not. You would not want to send me on a junket to help solve the global economic crisis, although I recognize the problem and can support those who have been gifted with the preparation, knowledge, and experience to deal with such issues. Even though I am a trained social worker and commissioned minister, I am not the person you would most want to provide one-on-one counseling, although I can do it. I am better at enabling others to work one-on-one. The word that keeps flashing through my mind as I think about this continuum of caring and being a part of the body of Christ is *interdependence*.

Interdependence

Our interdependence was best illustrated when God sent a baby as our source of salvation. Think about that. It is a relationship that is very unequal yet more than equal. Similarly, God turned Jesus' death into our source of life. Mary and Joseph were called to nurture and love the hope of the world. Today, we as disciples of Christ are called to nurture love and spread hope in the world. That can only happen when we learn to walk the tightrope of interdependence and accept the reality that what we do impacts, positively or negatively, God's other children, and that what they do impacts us. We are called to maintain or at least move toward a balance that serves the common good for all. The government of the United States of America has translated that into the lofty purpose of ensuring liberty and justice for all its citizens. The nation of God has been charged with reaching for an even higher level of commitment described as loving our neighbor as we love ourselves. We Christians who are from the United States are called to do both. We do neither when we wage war with each other, trying to use our government to legislate our beliefs on others.

I routinely hear that our country was founded by persons seeking religious freedom, which is certainly true for some of the founders. If most Americans were to spend much time researching their genealogy, they would find a lot of folks who came here on a lark, in search of fortune, or to avoid imprisonment. Many of those who came for religious freedom were not necessarily concerned about anybody else's religious freedom. They wanted to worship the way they had determined was the right way and really probably wanted everybody else to worship like them. Our religious freedom, which I strongly believe to be a good thing, resulted from having to pull together for the common good against others who wanted to control us in general. Even though it probably resulted from expediency rather than a great vision of religious freedom, our philosophy as a country has become a shining light in the world. We do not want to put that light out.

What we can do is work with the various levels of government, allowing the government to do the things that they are better designed to do toward ensuring the common good and filling the gaps in this continuum of caring, in most instances without constraint to our basic beliefs. I have had the great privilege of working with Catholic nuns who truly mourn the very existence of abortion, but whose lives have been dedicated to assuring that pregnant women and all children with whom they come into contact are loved and nurtured. It has always seemed somewhat ironic to me that the people who do not believe in capital punishment are most often the people not only ministering to prisoners, but also to the victims of crime. There is a niche for each of us who call ourselves Christians on this continuum of caring. All we need to do is seek, and we will find it.

CHAPTER 9
EXPLORING THE OTHER PURPOSES OF THE UNITED STATES

> I am not at all concerned about that, that the Lord is on our side in this great struggle, for I know that the Lord is always on the side of the right; but it is my constant anxiety and prayer that I and this nation may be on the Lord's side.
> —Abraham Lincoln

Establish Justice

The Merriam-Webster dictionary gives the following definitions of the word *just*[20]:

- having a basis in or conforming to fact or reason
- conforming to a standard of correctness, proper
- acting or being in conformity with what is morally upright or good, righteous
- being what is merited, deserved

To establish justice, then, the government of the United States is charged with the responsibility of setting forth laws that are reasonable and proper and establishing laws that spell out a means of rectifying situations where what is reasonable and proper has not occurred. The problem is that we have differing opinions regarding what is reasonable and proper as well as what constitutes a failure to comply with such laws. Our founders recognized this dilemma by establishing a system of checks and balances among our legislative, executive, and judicial government branches, charging them each to be vigilant regarding the reasonableness and properness of governance. I am a strong supporter of these checks and balances, but even they have experienced thorny times. We the people are, in the final analysis, the keepers of justice, as we hold our elected and appointed officials accountable for their actions or lack thereof.

The real challenge regarding justice is the one in the middle of the definitions listed above: What is right? It is the question that seems to get left out of deliberations most of the time. Determining what is right requires thoughtful consideration weighing all of the known consequences of one act over another and trying to project the unknown. This is really hard to do in the midst of powerful lobbyists who have blinders on regarding supporting anything other than what impacts them.

I have been blessed over the last thirty years to be in a Sunday school class with people from a broad spectrum of life, but particularly important for me are the people who operate small businesses. They give me a better picture from which to form my opinions about a subject about which I know very little. A few times in recent years my church has utilized a process of dialogue called World Café[21] that enables conversation among diverse sectors of the population. For example, we discussed health care before the Affordable Care Act was passed. Our group included doctors, nurses, insurance agents, uninsured persons, young adults, and senior citizens. We were not pressured to make any final conclusions but to listen and learn from one another. We came away from the process with a much clearer understanding of the problem and the possible solutions. We came away better prepared citizens of the United States. Most forums for the public are conducted by one side or the other on an issue, which does not allow for this kind of openness. The church that is brave enough to sponsor open meetings such as these, without telling people what they should think, would be contributing to the common good. Jesus challenged us "to let your light shine before others, so that they may see your good works and give glory to your Father in heaven" (Matthew 5:16). I cannot think of a better subject to shine a light on than justice.

Ensure Domestic Tranquility

> It is neither wealth nor splendor, but tranquility and occupation which give happiness.
> —Thomas Jefferson

> The Constitution is never tested during times of tranquility; it is during times of tension, turmoil, tragedy, trauma, and terrorism that it is sorely tested.
> —Amaury de Barros Conti

> But I have calmed and quieted my soul,
> like a weaned child with its mother;
> my soul is like the weaned child that is with me.
> —Psalm 131:2

Actually, I had not read the Constitution for some time and had forgotten that "[ensure] domestic tranquility" was even in it. Tranquility to me is related to God. It refers to internal peace and is a part of that steady state of resting in and with God. *Tranquility* is not even a word we use much anymore. Has it lost its luster?

Houses Divided

When I was a child, we had a neighbor who walked up and down the roads—all day, every day, it seemed. She was mentally ill and lived on a farm a few miles from us. We kids were afraid of her. She would walk into our driveway, and my mom would see her coming and open the screen door, inviting her to come in and sit at the kitchen table. Mom would give her a cold drink of water and make small talk about how hot or cold it was outside, how the crops were doing, and what she was doing at the time. Our neighbor never looked at Mom, and I do not remember the neighbor ever saying a word. Mom would refill her glass when it got empty. Almost like magic, the neighbor would suddenly stand up and leave without saying good-bye or anything. One day when we three children were in the house alone (Mom was probably in the garden, and Dad was most likely on a tractor in a nearby field), one of us thought we saw this neighbor coming. We hid in closets and whispered back and forth, "Do you think she is gone yet?" I do not think we ever told our parents what we had done, but our domestic tranquility had been threatened, whether in reality or in our imaginations.

What did the founders mean by "[ensure] domestic tranquility"? In its simplest form, this means to be able to be at home in peace and quiet without fear. At the time of the founding of this country, riots in the streets were common. The Boston Tea Party was a riot of sorts. We need to step back in time and understand what was going on in this country when these words were added to the Constitution. War was still in our founders' backyards. Disease was rampant, and material goods were scarce. If common people wanted a chair to sit in, they built it out of a tree they cut down. The common good demanded that commerce be developed, health care and sanitation be available, and alliances be formed with the natives with whom they shared this land. Peace and quiet would have been a luxury indeed. Freedom from fear truly rested with God.

Today, we probably are more concerned about terrorists or the senseless shootings that have occurred at schools and other public places. These are genuine concerns. I was sitting in my office at the Oklahoma state capitol complex some twenty blocks from the Alfred P. Murrah Federal Office Building on April 19, 1995, the day it was bombed at 9:02 a.m. I did not feel a thing, but as if on cue, every person who was sitting in the open area outside my office jumped and called out, "What was that?" At 6:00 a.m., I had swum at the YMCA located directly to the northeast of that building. The Y building was also destroyed, and several of the children in the day care center located in it were injured.

I had a pressing need to do something, anything, and when they called for blood donors, I quickly jumped in my car and found the nearest donation station. There were hundreds of donors in line. Apparently, we all felt the need to help. A few days later we learned that they actually got more blood than was immediately needed because so many of the victims had died.[22]

The lesson I gleaned from this experience is that the United States and all the faith groups located in it must answer that call to do something proactive about ensuring domestic tranquility. We must heal the divisions that separate us and reach out to the alienated loners starting in preschool and never stopping. If ever there was a call to love our neighbors as we love ourselves, it sounded throughout the world on April 19, 1995.

I am privileged to serve on the Oklahoma Coalition to Abolish the Death Penalty with Bud Welch and Jannie Coverdale. Bud's daughter, Julie Marie, was killed in the bombing, as were Jannie's grandsons, Aaron and Elijah. Both of these beautiful people, Bud and Jannie, spend much of their lives building bridges to prevent needless deaths, including those of the perpetrators. Bud says that his faith excluded capital punishment but his daughter's death was so traumatic he was having trouble dealing with it. He finally contacted Timothy McVeigh's [23] father and went to visit him. What he found was another father, just like him, in disbelief and pain. From that experience grew Bud's call to care and make a difference.

I fear, however, that many of us have become somewhat complacent about the world we live in. We are more like my brother, sister, and me hiding from our mentally ill neighbor than like my mother, who lived her love. Please understand I do think we need to be prudent in safety. Children should not open the door to strangers. In all honesty, our preventing something from happening is as helpful to the disenfranchised as it is to us. Timothy McVeigh would not have been executed and might have gotten the help he needed had we been able to prevent the Oklahoma City bombing.

Yet the whole idea of ensuring domestic tranquility does not simply mean that we have to have our baggage scanned at airports or the police check on the neighbors when their party gets too loud. Ensuring domestic tranquility requires us to plumb deeply into the causes of the lack of tranquility for every citizen and to address those causes with justice and freedom for all.

Oklahoma has strict laws legislating the registration of convicted sex offenders and where they can and cannot live. These laws may be prudent, but they markedly limit the futures of those who have offended. A ministry was developed in Oklahoma City to address the needs of sex offenders leaving prison and to protect the public, particularly children, from future problems. The ministry was located in a trailer park well away from places designated as off-limits to this population. It was a voluntary entrance program, where the offenders submitted themselves to close supervision. It, however, was unwanted by the nearby neighbors and consequently was zoned out of existence. Now some of the offenders are living on the streets. Where is the domestic tranquility in that?

Bullying segues to loss of domestic tranquility. A neighbor of one of my nephews had a ten-year-old son who was being bullied at school, apparently relentlessly. It is my understanding that one day he stood up to the bully, and the school suspended the son. When he got home, he killed himself. His dad now works tirelessly to end bullying, but his dad will never have domestic tranquility again.

None of this is easy. There is a fine line in legislation between too little and too much. We as a country certainly overreacted when we moved our Japanese citizens to internment camps during World War II. Our elected officials are not the only ones who must get involved in finding solutions. Elected officials always do better when they have a well-informed electorate who take the time to consider all sides of issues and support their representatives when they take the road of a statesperson, seeking what is best for the whole country or state, rather than kick the representatives out of office because they did not respond with knee-jerk, yet popular, reactions.

We face different challenges than our founders did, but the need for ensuring domestic tranquility should not be relegated to antiquity, nor should it be limited to threats and menaces. We all need to work together so that every family can come together over dinner with adequate food for all present and share their experiences of the day in peace and quiet without fear.

Provide for the Common Defense

> Every gun that is made, every warship launched, every rocket fired, signifies in the final sense a theft from those who hunger and are not fed, those who are cold and are not clothed.
> —Dwight D. Eisenhower

> I must study politics and war that my sons may have liberty to study mathematics and philosophy.
> —John Adams

> Ours is a world of nuclear giants and ethical infants. We know more about war than we know about peace, more about killing than we know about living.
> —Omar N. Bradley

> He shall judge between the nations,
> and shall arbitrate for many peoples;
> they shall beat their swords into ploughshares,
> and their spears into pruning-hooks;
> nation shall not lift up sword against nation,
> neither shall they learn war any more.
> —Isaiah 2:4

I long for a world that does not know war. I cannot say that I am an absolute pacifist yet, but military intervention is becoming more and more untenable to me every day. I have been skipping this purpose of our Constitution; I am not the right person to discuss it. When I read what some of our generals thought about war, I think they are the ones to whom we should listen. Whether I like it or not, I do want to be protected, probably more importantly I want my brother and sister, their spouses, and my nieces and nephews and their families protected. At this writing, PBS routinely runs pictures of the soldiers killed in action in Afghanistan, honoring them in silence at the end of the nightly news. I have started praying for each of them and their families as their pictures appear. There is not much else I can do for them now.

I practiced counting, before I started school, by placing my figure on each of the still-evident pieces of shrapnel lining my Uncle Harvey's arms, saying, "One, two, three …" He seemed to get a kick out of it. He came home from WWII blind in one eye with metal plates in his head and in one leg. I never heard him talk about how it happened. My dad told us his brother was one of the first few guys in his platoon who made it across a bridge behind German lines before the bridge was blown and the others were killed. As injured as he was, he and one other guy walked back, making their way toward Allied forces. I do not see any way we could have avoided WWII. Is evil really so intractable? Where is love in war? Or, perhaps more importantly, how can we love in war?

This I know: providing for the common defense should not be driven by pride or feelings of superiority. The United States does have a superior military and certainly has dedicated soldiers, but England had a superior military when we won the Revolutionary War. Yes, their military was stretched thin at the time, and we had help from the French, but we had more to lose than they did. War and our defense must be focused on ending the need for war. Surely providing for the common defense includes building bridges of peace and seeking to assure that there is no other nation or people in the world who has more to lose than we do.

Secure the Blessings of Liberty to Ourselves and Our Posterity

Our purpose as a nation calls us to provide for liberty for our children and our children's children, and perhaps to anyone we might influence. I heard an NPR report recently on constitutions being written in developing democracies. The people being interviewed noted that many things that are not in our Constitution are being added to the newer ones. But then one interviewee added that the US Constitution was the primer from which all started. One thing being added is protection of human rights. As grandparents learn from their grandchildren, we too might learn from our developing neighbors.

The constitutionally stated purposes of the federal government share a trait: they all are designed to work toward the common good. In the final analysis, I believe that trait is what sets all governments apart from the private sector, and recognizing that trait is paramount to our making any sense out of government functions. In the beginning of this nation, if roads connected a settler to a neighbor or an area of commerce, individuals or families developed them themselves. They probably at some point worked something out with a neighbor, which resulted in several neighbors getting together and hiring someone else to maintain the road. That, my friends, eventually developed into an entity to oversee the road maintenance, and the need for government arose.

The common good always relates to our interdependence. While we are a nation of great individualists, we need each other. And we need to elect officials who are more dedicated to ensuring the common good for all than to implementing any specific ideology or solely supporting any special interest.

CHAPTER 10
GOVERNMENT AND PRODUCTIVITY

Having worked for a state government where my tasks usually related to implementing federal programs, I can tell you that governments can never be operated like businesses. While businesses may have neat little phrases that state their purpose in advertisements, every commercial business has one purpose: to make a profit. Although some choose to, businesses are not required to ever worry about the common good. Thus, laying off staff, shutting down a plant, and moving to a different location are all appropriate actions to take to ensure that the company continues to make a profit. I am not being critical or cynical; that is just the way it is.

In the early 1980s the United States as a whole was experiencing an economic downturn while Oklahoma was awash in oil. There were actually a few states that bought their welfare recipients one-way bus tickets to Oklahoma, giving them the opportunity to take advantage of the ready employment here. They clearly did not understand the nature of work in the oil field, as most of those sent were women with children, who came to the Department of Human Services in Oklahoma for help.

As we have recently experienced, such economic bubbles do burst. The ultimate bust of the Oklahoma economy is usually attached to the failure of Penn Square Bank in July 1982. The following recession that struck Oklahoma severely eroded our tax base. Our state government was looking for every way possible to meet the ever-increasing needs of the people within the context of this shrinking source of revenue. By 1985, our budget at the Department of Human Services was cut to the extent that every employee had to take a pay cut of either 5 or 7.5 percent while working with, by that time, record caseloads. Staff grumbled about being taxed at a higher rate than other state citizens, although no one else called our pay cuts a tax but us. All of us, from the front-line worker to the director, knew that our services were literally accounting for more and more of the population just having food to eat, and so we trudged on as we had been taught good public servants did. Because of the breadth of the purpose of government, it is impossible to apply standard business practices designed to ensure profits to address the issues of meeting the common good. In some ways government serves as a necessary counterbalance to commerce's profit-seeking ways.

One of the challenges governments face, however, is being efficient and effective when the singularity of purpose of making a profit does not exist. In the early 1990s, Oklahoma took a long hard look at its child care delivery systems. Child care is provided by a mix of for-profit and nonprofit businesses ranging from large national chains to an individual in his or her own home. DHS is responsible for not only licensing these facilities, but also administering various child care subsidy programs. The largest part of child care is provided in small businesses, many of which needed to get the subsidy check for the children included in these programs before the child care facility could make its payroll each month.

The governor heard the industry's complaints, primarily about our failure to get these checks out in a timely manner, and DHS was told to fix it. I drew the dubious task of bringing industry leaders and DHS staff together in monthly meetings to identify problems and address them. We generally found good intent on the part of DHS but in many instances bad results. DHS took pride in never having missed a delivery of welfare checks to thousands of Oklahomans by the first of each month for over fifty years. When we applied the same system to payment of child care subsidies, we found it was not practical. For one thing, we were putting a check for each child in an individual envelope and mailing it to the day care provider. A facility with one hundred children receiving child care subsidy got one hundred envelopes. Some of them had to hire staff to just open, record, and deposit these checks! Who knew? Believe me, once identified, that problem was quickly addressed, not only helping the facilities but also saving the costs of stamps and envelopes. Today children are signed in to care each day electronically, and payment is made by direct deposit. It took the dedicated effort of the child care industry and the state agency to together reach the common good.

The solution to such inefficiency does not lie in the private sector. I personally have longed for a governor to call to correct mistreatment by private businesses but have not yet found one. The solution lies in good relationships between the public and private sectors, continuous commitment to improvement, and the dedication and character of those public employees.

Contracting for Governmental Services

Government, perhaps because it has not been as diligent as it should have been about efficiency and effectiveness, has turned to the private sector through contracting for services. However, I believe government in some instances has been scapegoated as inept and inefficient so that more money can be passed through to the private sector. This push to privatize largely accounts for much of the corruption in government expenditures and among lobbyists and elected officials.

One of the actions that is often taken to make government more "productive" is to invite supposedly unbiased private sector "experts," to evaluate practices and make recommendations. One particular study in which I was involved required hours and hours of state employee staff time to compile data for the study. The state staff essentially did all the work except writing the conclusions. We had staff members who were more than qualified to analyze the data, but we were deemed biased. The report we got back was a standard boilerplate of recommendation to cut staff and consolidate programs. The first problem we noted was that the number of counties stated in the report was wrong. We thought that might be a typo. Several pieces of data were also quoted wrong. Then we noticed that some programs it recommended we consolidate did not exist in Oklahoma. We checked and discovered that the last similar report this company had done was for Georgia, which did have the number of counties noted and the programs we did not have. The company had apparently not even bothered to change the language. The state paid, if I remember correctly, $250,000 for that study, and the powers that be who ordered the study ignored our concerns that the study was factually incorrect. It did not matter. The researchers knew what recommendations they were supposed to make before they started. Many of the recommendations were implemented. Staff reductions occurred across the board.

This was really an assault on state employees that continues to this day. Oklahoma was recently sued for failure to comply with even basic child welfare services. According to newspaper reports, staff-to-family ratios were way off. Even before I left, I was beginning to understand more clearly what the Israelites went through when they were required to make more and more bricks with fewer and fewer resources. I do not think Oklahoma is unique in this regard, and the federal government may now be under similar assault.

The history of the beginning of public welfare programs in America actually started in the nineteenth century, when the Industrial Revolution was drawing more and more people to cities. The new industries did not need all who came. Individuals were injured on the job, and their families were left to their own resources. When a breadwinner was unemployed, injured, or killed, the family was left on their own. City governments' first response was to contract for services, but officials soon discovered that the contractors were more interested in making money than caring for people in need. They were providing only the most basic of help, if that, and keeping the rest of the money for themselves. Sounds like the tax collectors in the New Testament. Thus, public employees were hired and charged with the solemn trust of providing for the common good, which they did. This most likely was the same start for other types of public employment. These people, recruited for their integrity and dedication to service, were paid reasonable wages and good benefits to step out of the private sector and meet the common good. It seems we have come full circle.

Not only are some consultative, business-based activities harmful to governmental functioning, but the whole process of contracting is fraught with mischief as well. The staff members who prepare the announcement for bidding a contract must be at least as knowledgeable as the people bidding for the contract. In other words, a government entity must have staff to prepare the contract so those bidding the contract know exactly what is expected. For example, when requesting contracted services to develop customized computer software, the contract has to be so specific that an expert in the field has to write it.

Contractors also develop bids to include very specific deliverables. In my state the lowest and best bid must be selected. Many times, I worked with contractors who got the bid based on the lowest and best bid only to find out later in the development process that their careful wording of the document based on their interpretation meant some major aspect was not included, which usually resulted in a modification of the contract, increasing the payment above what some other entity had bid. When the cost of writing and processing contracts is added to the cost of the contract—including in most instances a profit by the contractor—the cost of the project almost always exceeds what it would have cost to do the work internally.

There are, of course, many things that the government should purchase through contract, but that too can be a challenge. I remember one time asking my administrative assistant to procure an adding machine for me that had a hard-copy tape. (Remember, I started working before personal computers.) She came back with the report that the cheapest one on the list of preapproved adding machines cost $250—and that was in the 1970s. I bought an adding machine for $10 at a local office supply store. I used that same adding machine until I retired in 2004 and brought it home when I retired. I rarely used it after I got a computer—but really, $250?

Checks and balances are important and needed throughout government. Oklahoma solved the problem to some extent when it implemented a program making the preapproved listing available but allowing an item at a lower price to be purchased instead. If nothing else, that rule cleaned up the preapproved bid list.

CHAPTER 11
COMMONLY HELD VALUES

Government most often takes its form from commonly held values. In such instances, rules and laws sculpt structure for the ease of implementing what is held as the common good. Indeed, most government functions continue rather seamlessly without much thought. If I pay my monthly bill, water comes out when I turn on a faucet. Two or three times over the past thirty years, I have received a postcard from the city telling me that the level of some contaminate was elevated but remained below levels deemed dangerous. The card would indicate that I would be notified if action was needed. My city government is at work doing what it is supposed to do in support of my desire to have safe drinking water, and I take that for granted every time I get a glass of water—and I should be able to take it for granted.

Problems arise in regard to government when one group's values are not the values of other groups and when rules or laws that are developed to support the one group's values interfere with the way of life of the other group. The enactment of the prohibition of the sale of alcohol in the early twentieth century is an example of structure being put in place where not enough people shared the relevant values to make it viable. It is not hard to understand the concern of those who saw lives being wasted by alcoholism or innocent lives being lost due to damage resulting from alcohol misuse. Nor is it difficult to see the lack of fairness on the part of all those who drank responsibly being forbidden to drink at all. Thus, prohibition was repealed. Smoking is another issue with similar challenges but with the added belief that secondhand smoke is very dangerous. While recognizing an individual's right to smoke, seeking the common good has resulted in laws being created to protect others from smoke, and warnings have been applied to tobacco to alert smokers of the potential problems resulting from use of tobacco. Democracies are grounded in the ability of elected representatives to negotiate compromises like these.

When governmental issues deal with areas that are also faith issues for some, those individuals and groups have the right to make their preferences known just like any other individual or group and to suggest possible compromises. There were many faith groups involved on both sides during the Prohibition.

I, for one, do not believe that any person convicted of a crime should be executed, a stance I base on my belief that God is the only one who can pass final judgment on anyone. I am a member of a group that agrees that capital punishment is wrong, but others in it may not share my reasoning or be coming from a faith stance at all. There are religious groups that support capital punishment, and there are people who do not support capital punishment who have no religious affiliation. Capital punishment was actually ended in the United States during the twentieth century for a while, but that law was overturned. Capital punishment is legal and used in my state and by the federal government. I will continue my efforts to end capital punishment while continuing to support my government. Until more people take on the value that no one should be executed, capital punishment will continue.

Isn't that exactly what Paul did as he traversed between Jerusalem and Asia Minor, working to mold disparate peoples into one body of Christ? He was trying to find a common denominator for the continuation of the nation of God among all the peoples of the earth. Finding the core that really matters is rather like eating an artichoke. We find a little food on the petals, but the heart of the food is underneath them. Before we can find that common core with all God's children, we have to recognize what is a petal and what is real food in our own belief systems. There may not be anything wrong with our petal; it might just be different from others. The food of God's love is the same on all of the petals. Paul continued to follow Jewish practices throughout his life. They apparently were meaningful to him, just as the non-Jewish practices of his new siblings in Christ became for him.

The art of compromise in a democracy is driven by the common good. When we can keep that at the center of the table, productive discourse can occur.

With this background on church and state, let us take a closer look at our economy and then flesh out specific wedge issues dividing church and state today.

CHAPTER 12
THE ECONOMY

The United States is in an economic mess—as is the world, for that matter—and there are no easy fixes. It will take at least one decade and probably two just to move from where we are now to reach an adequate state. My first recommendation, therefore, is to chill out. Our need for instant gratification is making matters worse with our Chicken Little[24] reactions to every new piece of information that is released. While some on Wall Street may get a rush from seeing if they can capitalize on the missed calls of others, the rest of us do not have to listen to them or walk in lockstep with them. It is sort of like losing weight. Most of us did not gain weight overnight, and I can promise you from personal experience that it cannot be lost overnight. Actually, many of the quick weight loss ideas do more harm than good. We all know how to lose weight: eat less and exercise more. But in all honesty, it takes a complete change in our character and values to eat less and exercise more. We will never be able to go back to our old habits. It may not be fair that others can seem to eat all they want, never lift a weight, and never gain a pound, but that is the way it is, and my not liking it is not going to change it.

Likewise, we know how to solve the problems in our economy: we need to live within our means, and we need to have a plan to cover unexpected expenses to deal with the normal ebbs and flows of life and business cycles. And here, too, we must face the fact that our character and values are the driving forces behind our economic failures and realize that changing our values and character is the only thing that can save our economy. We seem to have lost our collective conscience. Where have integrity and honesty gone? Integrity is not making sure you have included a clause in the fine print of a multi-paged mortgage describing in complex legalese that a loan includes a balloon payment that would be devastating to anybody in three or four years. It leaves me breathless just reading about it. Honesty is not merely remaining silent when the truth is being tested.

Church is not much help here, either, for it is as guilty as the rest in not practicing integrity and honesty. From sex abuse scandals to fraudulent use of funds to merely failing to act, the church gives moral credence to character lapses. We in the church sometimes like to cover character lapses with self-righteousness, which is just as harmful. In general, we know the difference between right and wrong. God created us with that capacity. We actually have to work counter to our nature to become indifferent to right and wrong and to ignore this basic ingredient of our being. It is that habit development that we have to change.

While the economic problems started with us individually and collectively, they eventually reached the point where the government had to intercede in the fall of 2008 to avoid catastrophe. The actual misdeeds of some, accompanied by the tacit approval of more, have pushed our economic failure into the category of causing damage to the common good. Thus far, we the people, through our representative government, have applied some short-term bandages. I pray it is not too little too late. Now we need to get about the business of long-range fixes.

As with an individual, family, or business, our government at all levels must identify and provide the essentials for protecting the common good while reaching a point where our income supports outgo and plans exist for the unexpected. That lofty goal must be reached within complex systemic change, where each action can have unintended consequences. Some of these unintended consequences might be good, but others might not. Yes, we do need to reduce the national debt, but that cannot be done by merely making government leaner. Actually, government reductions of staff at all levels account to some degree for slowing down the economy, as it results in increased unemployment. Yes, we do need to make government as trim and lean as possible, but we need to do it over time and when appropriate.

I once drew the assignment of guiding a simulation that brought together some of our best and brightest high school students to lead them in the process of allocating human services funding. The exercise started with a presentation of what the services do and whom they impact. It ends with the students having to decide, for example, whether funding should go to caring for the elderly or for children, for food stamps or Medicaid, or for child welfare intervention or child support collection. It is mind-boggling. And never did we ever get to the point of addressing the real questions: which of these services provide for the common good, and how should that impact how we spend money?

Constituencies and the Common Good

In regard to governmental work, each of these programs comes with its own constituencies. Did you know the food stamp program is not a human service or welfare program at all and never has been? It is a farm supplement program created to help impact the price of farm commodities. It remains assigned to the Committee on Agriculture in Congress (although that status is under debate). The ever-increasing number of persons over the age of sixty-five creates a powerful lobby for services for the elderly. The groups with vested interest in Medicaid and Medicare are too numerous to list. Children do not have many powerful and well-funded lobbyists, but I doubt seriously that is because we do not need to help children to ensure the common good.

What I have described is just one very small part of the whole picture of federal responsibilities. Most of the big lobbyists do not hang around human services. When I went to welfare conferences, someone might be handing out bags of peanuts or ink pens with someone's logo on them, or we might have been invited to a cheese-and-crackers party sponsored by groups that were usually nonprofits that legally cannot lobby. Since I worked with data, I had opportunities to attend a few data conferences and get a glimpse of bigger-time lobbying with Hawaiian luaus and boot-scooting buddies. Imagine how our representatives who deal with military funding or create laws related to oil and gas might be treated.

The only thing that can distract our representatives from this kind of treatment is our votes. Yet Americans have quit voting. In the 2012 primary, my precinct had a 10 percent turnout. If we vote, we must take it upon ourselves to be well informed. The outrageous amount of anonymous money being poured into campaigns over the past few years, I believe, will burn itself out over time, but in the meantime, we are being inundated with even more half-truths and comments taken out of context than is present in a normal election cycle. These are all designed to gut-punch us in subtle ways that in most instances have absolutely nothing to do with the candidate's stance on an issue or qualification for office.

Take the time to identify the most unbiased sources possible and follow them. You are an important piece in the solutions of the problems we face. Would you buy a house or a car based on the ads you see on TV or the scary fear mongering e-mails circulating through your social network, church, or relatives? I do not think so. Neither should you vote for someone without more facts. Remember, honesty and integrity are sorely missing. And keep an eye on that old nemesis, instant gratification. If it sounds too good to be true, it probably is.

Australia[25] solves the problem of lack of voter participation by fining any one eligible to vote for not voting. Now there is a clever way to raise money to reduce the national debt! Of course, that would mean we want everyone who is eligible to vote to do so. It seems to me that political parties really only want their core constituents to vote. I must confess that when you think about the information the vast majority of eligible voters have on which to make such decisions, it is with some fear and trembling that I consider the results of an election where everyone who is eligible to vote does.

I doubt if we will ever get to the point of fining people for not voting, but increasing taxes will be necessary. It is not true that all citizens do not want to pay taxes. I for one do not mind paying my fair share of taxes. The problem arises in defining what is fair.

A Living Wage

Our society has been morphing for the past decades into a service society. The use of services has become a way of life for most of us. Even if we add more high-paying jobs or, more likely, *because* we add more high paying jobs, the demand for the service industries will continue and grow. Actually, some of the jobs in the service industry are well paid: accountants, lawyers, doctors, plumbers, electricians, etc. Others may not be, such as fast-food servers, nannies, child care workers, nursing assistants, and store clerks. Anyone who works full-time deserves to earn a living wage.[26] Many of us did these jobs on our way through school headed toward those "better-paying" jobs. Who knows? If we actually paid high school and college students a living wage, they might even be able to graduate from college without owing their souls to student loans.

I enjoyed being a waitress and a nurse's aide. I have many times said I learned more about management watching the boss where I was a waitress than I learned in all the classes I had in graduate school. For many, however, such service jobs will be a reality throughout their careers. The vast majority of the people in those high-paying jobs do not want these service providers to go away. Service employees have just as much right to be self-supportive in what they do as anybody else. The minimum wage is a joke at $15,080 per year as of 2012. It is just below the poverty guidelines for a family of two, $15,130. Once Social Security (employees pay 6.2 percent as of 2013) and Medicare (employee pays 1.45 percent) are deducted, it becomes $13,922.55. This assumes that the individual worked forty hours each week for all fifty-two weeks of the year, which rarely would happen. Many of these employees do not get sick leave or vacation leave. Many of them are not scheduled to work a full forty hours.

Let us say you and one other family member, most often now a minor child, are earning $13,922.55 per year, $1,160.21 per month. How are you going to make ends meet? You will most likely have to rely on food stamps[27], Medicaid, and a child care subsidy. If you ever get a raise, it will be deducted from these supplements until eventually you will max out on eligibility and totally fall off an economic cliff, potentially leaving you in worse shape than when you got the job in the first place. It is a bleak existence.

The ratio of average worker pay to CEO pay has grown obscene in recent years.[28] The poverty level in the United States has increased during this downturn in the economy to 15.1 percent. Just as sad is the marked increase in the persons with earned incomes, who are now bringing home salaries at or near the poverty level.[29] Beyond wage inequities, our tax system is structured with breaks that for all practical purposes are more readily applicable to the wealthy than to the middle class. Thus, the middle class largely ends up footing the bill for these wage supplements, provided to offset what businesses are not paying service workers.

I know of no clearer data illustrating that what is supposed to trickle down does not. Many times over the past several years when I listen to the news about our economy I am reminded of the Hans Christian Andersen's story *The Emperor's New Clothes*[30]. I guess people do not read stories like that anymore—or is it that we just do not learn from them?

My strong personal belief is that people should make at least enough money to eat and have clothing and shelter. I have moved into the category of those who believe that health care falls in the category of the common good and thus meets the criteria of being a shared burden. I am very close to adding child care to that list. I find it fascinating that the business community has not demanded these services. Most of the industrialized world offers governmentally supported health care and child care, creating a skewed disadvantage for the United States regarding international trade. The United States actually offered some excellent government sponsored child care for Rosie the Riveter[31] during World War II. I guess we are more pragmatic when we are fighting a common enemy, not each other.

I am just enough of a capitalist, however, to think that the government should not have to supplement wages to support businesses that are thriving. People who work fulltime and meet the job requirements should earn a living wage. Getting there from where we are now is the tough part. A total revamping of our tax system designed to support a living wage for all workers would probably be the place to start. For example, the primary exemption from paying business income taxes for businesses with low-wage employees might be based on the number of employees being paid a living wage.

Work

Where do young people learn how to work today? There are people who for whatever reason are truly unable to work because of age or disability. We do, I believe, as a nation have a responsibility to ensure that these people live as meaningful a life as possible in a safe and nurturing environment, but the rest of us must work for a living, and therefore we all must be trained to work. That training includes not only a particular skill or body of knowledge, but also the understanding that work equals self-support and family support. Because work does not currently equal self-support and family support, we are raising an entire generation of young people who out of necessity must develop great skills in accessing assistance. They must invest time and energy in this process that could be applied to enhancing their career potentials. I was in the church office recently when a very fine-looking, well-groomed, well-mannered young man who I would guess was about eighteen came in and asked if this was the place that gave out gas coupons. His mother had told him that he could get a coupon at the church. His mother is trying to teach him how to survive in the only why she knows how.

I grew up on a farm. I joke about being put in charge of chickens when I was five years old. To my urban colleagues that is funny, but it is also true. On a small, rather self-sustaining farm, children cut their teeth on some type of chore. I thought it was fun to carry in the kindling wood with my dad when he brought in large armloads of cut-up logs for use in heating our home. It was a rite of passage when I reached the ripe old age of five and could be trusted to gather the eggs and feed the chickens—my mother was close by, but I did the work. I have actually lived in urban areas for most of my adult life. And I must tell you—I left the farm with no regrets; I liked the animals but hated working in the garden. I have also always found it rather amusing that women in the workforce were somehow deemed a new phenomenon from the 1960s onward. They ought to have followed my mom around for a day or two. I am, however, thankful that I learned how to work from my early life experience. That way of life still exists in places across the farmlands of America today, but it is a dying lifestyle. What has taken its place in our industrialized and digitized world?

As we industrialized and migrated from farm to city, we became more interdependent. Work became more specialized, requiring targeted training. That specialization is still evolving—in the service industries, for example.

There has never been a time when education has been more important. I remember as a small child listening to the news about the integration of the Little Rock school system and seeing the angry mobs protesting busing. My dad had to drop out of school after the eighth grade, because he had to go to work to help support his recently widowed mother and brothers and sisters, but also because there was no transportation into town, where he would have had to go for high school. He could not even imagine people being upset about having to ride a bus to school. I think it was also beyond my father's imagination to use the color of one's skin as criteria of worth, but that is another story.

I don't know what has happened to education. Is it just that so many of us are aging that we have lost sight of the fact that an educated citizenry is a prerequisite for a flourishing democracy? We are all responsible for ensuring that everyone from birth to the grave is growing in spirit and in truth. That demands the basic abilities to understand history, geography, and science and to read, write, do math, use money, live healthily, interact with others, and, most importantly, how to reason and think. Education is always for the common good. Let me say that again: education is always for the common good. I am certainly not an expert on learning, but it is clear that we are not where we need to be in this area. What I do know is that in a democracy, quality public education is essential. It seems that the income transfer that has been occurring in our society for the past forty years from the poor to the wealthy has resulted in some loss of lessons on values and character that are fundamental to our society thriving as a democracy. Some remedial work may be needed, and parents may need to be taught so they can teach these lessons to their children.

I sat at the table at an end-of-the-school-year celebration with the mother of the ten-year-old girl I was tutoring and watched the mother's bright, inquisitive two-year-old play nearby. He was calling out the colors and pointing to them on the toy he had. His mother had tears in her eyes when she looked at me and said, "My daughter never had a chance to learn her colors when she was two." The mother had been a teenager when the oldest child was born. Her husband was out of the picture before the youngest was born. The mother had had to apply for welfare, was placed in a good work-training program, and was now working for the first time in her life. Her son learned his colors in child care, but the mother also now had the self-resources to support his learning and the will to grow and learn more herself. Obviously she also wanted the very best for her daughter, or she would not have been celebrating her progress from being tutored.

While digging around in my own genealogy, I found the indenture papers for my ancestor William Knott, who at the age of fifteen in 1788, was indentured to a Mr. Bagley to learn the trade of working with iron. The contract also included the prerequisite that during his seven-year tenure of servitude, he was to be taught how to read, write, and cipher. The heritage of our ancestors to support education is the reason I can read, write, and cipher today. My fifth-generation great-grandparent served as what was essentially a slave for seven years. He apparently learned his trade well and was successful as an employee at a steel forge in Pennsylvania. He even learned it well enough that instead of being drafted into the army for the War of 1812, he was conscripted to make rifles for soldiers. My sixth-generation great-grandparents had the foresight to see that their future and their child's future depended on their children getting an education. Do we?

We have created a culture of survival among our low-income citizens. In the time my parents spent teaching me how to work, these parents are teaching children how to survive on the streets. Their children are learning where to get help finding food, clothing, shelter, and transportation. Forcing people to live in an underground economy, we undergird dishonesty. For most of my career, I have dreamed of finding the answer to how to redirect some very good survivor skills into work skills. It is hard for those of us ensconced in our middle-class-ness to understand how hard it is to change one's whole way of being, which is what we are asking people with limited incomes to do. The best work I have seen over the years in trying to get a handle on this is *Bridges out of Poverty*,[32] and I would commend it to you for group study.

We sometimes forget that the Bible is the story of God's peoples, both good and bad. Early after the split in Israel, the boy king Josiah[33] came to rule. He hastened the repairs of the then damaged temple and in that process the book of the law was found. It was brought to the king, and he quickly realized that God's people had not been following God but had been developing their own religion. Now, the temple was still functioning. There were priests working and collections being taken. But somewhere in the process the basic tenets of their faith had been buried in the rubble. I wonder how far we have strayed from the tenets of our faith.

The problem, of course, is that we will never be able to start from scratch and create the utopia for which we long. We were, however, created with brains and hearts that God gave us to use in just such a time as this. With God's help, I think we might be surprised at what we can accomplish. Remember that Acts 1 leads into Acts 2.

CHAPTER 13
THE ISSUES THAT DIVIDE US: ABORTION

Abortion is one of the most divisive issues to hit the church in the last forty years. I want to share with you an experience that shaped my views on abortion, what those views are, and some ideas that might help the church find some common ground on which to build. I graduated from college in 1969 and that summer started my job with the Oklahoma Department of Human Services (Public Welfare at that time), where I actually only worked as a direct service provider for two years. I do not remember knowing a whole lot about abortion when I graduated, four years before Roe v. Wade.

During my two years of direct work with clients, I took a call from a local doctor who was very concerned about an eleven-year-old girl for whom he cared. I took the call because the family's public assistance case was assigned to me. I cannot tell you today whether I had actually even visited with the family at that time. It seems the doctor had determined that the eleven-year-old was pregnant. He had referred her to an obstetrician who confirmed the diagnosis, and both of the physicians felt very strongly that there was a great chance the young pregnant girl would not carry the baby to term, that her immature womb would be permanently damaged, that the baby would most likely have multiple health problems if it survived, and that the girl might die. It seems the girl had become pregnant before she had her first period. I did not know that was possible but was assured that girls often ovulate for a few months before they menstruate. I was also told that the family did not have a clue who the father was, as the girl had been sexually active for at least two years with various boys, including relatives. The doctors had met with the girl's mother and strongly encouraged her to let them perform an abortion, but the mother had refused. The physician that called me wondered if I would talk to the girl's mother and encourage her to change her mind. This was all legal at that time because the life of the mother was at risk. It came down to a question: which child do we save?

I made a home visit and met with the girl and her mother. The girl was eventually sent out to play, as she obviously did not have a clue about the conversation and was bored. The girl's mother was proud of her youngest child who had been so blessed by God. The pregnancy was a miracle in the mother's mind. If God could cause this miracle, God certainly could protect the girl's womb and the baby. When I asked her if she thought her eleven-year-old was mature enough to take full-time responsibility for an at-risk baby, she said she had thought about that. Her oldest daughter had just turned eighteen and had not been blessed with a baby yet, and so the girl's mother had decided to give this baby to the older daughter when it was born.

The baby was delivered at six months and survived the delivery but had multiple serious medical complications and suspected developmental delays. Although the eleven-year-old survived the delivery, her reproductive organs were severely damaged.

I left that situation with more questions than answers as both a Christian and a social worker. What was abundantly clear to me was that we had essentially lost two lives with that birth even though both the girl and the baby lived.

I do not know from where the mother in the family described drew her religious teachings, but I have since been very cognizant of the unintended consequences of what I call the culturalization of our faith. This occurs both inside and outside the church. Our practices are not always as well grounded in the ways of Jesus as we might think.

I also profoundly realize that there are no simple solutions to complex problems. Laws provide structure for societal norms; they do not create new norms or alter old ones. Most of the people living in poverty with whom I have had contact believe that abortion is a bad thing. They may not have much, but children are something they can have. I recently went with a group from my church to serve dinner and attend worship at a service for the homeless provided by local churches. When prayer requests were taken, one young teen asked the group to pray that she would get pregnant. She had been trying for several months. She had no place to live and no income. Another young woman asked for prayers that she could get her little girl back. Apparently she had left the child with a relative but had no home and no income, and the relative would not let her have the child. The solution of finding a job and a place to live had not entered her mind. The third prayer request came from a very pregnant teen who wanted a healthy baby. She was soon to deliver but had at that point never had any prenatal care.

By primarily focusing our attention on abortion, we, the church, and this country are being distracted from meeting the common good of children and their families. It is also diverting precious resources away from actually addressing the underlying issues that result in abortion.

So this is where I stand on abortion. Abortion is a medical procedure, and, just like with every medical procedure that deals with life and death, decisions about those procedures lie in the realm of medical practice and ethics. Abortion should be turned to as a last resort and as rarely as possible. Roe v. Wade sets well the legal parameters regarding abortion, and I accept that.

I believe strongly in the separation of church and state, and for those faith systems that have strong beliefs against abortion or birth control, I would fight hard for their right to follow that belief if ever any part of our government tried to make them use birth control or have an abortion. Equally, for those whose faith system supports birth control or abortion, I would fight hard if any part of our government tried to forbid any of these persons of faith from using birth control or having an abortion within the parameters of Roe v. Wade.

I have friends on both sides of this issue who will stop reading right now. I respectfully request that you read on, for I have a challenge for us all. I would like to call a moratorium on all activities related to dealing with abortion through legislation for five years and ask that all involved invest at least as much time and energy as they are currently expending regarding abortion in changing lives. I believe with all my heart that we can and will markedly reduce the number of abortions being performed if we take what we already know, learn more, and develop interventions to deal with the real issues. I also believe that there is a segment of our political community that jumps on the antiabortion bandwagon only because it delivers a block of voters no matter what else they are pushing. I do not believe that most of the good Christians who truly do not believe in abortion are also against prenatal care, child welfare, child nutrition, education, child care, and children's health, but they are supporting people who are at the least against providing adequate funding for these issues. One has to wonder why they care more about fetuses than breathing children. Why do they enforce carrying a fetus to term but not allocate funding for prenatal care and maternal nutrition?

What to Do during the Moratorium

The data quoted here is from the Guttmacher Institute, and I would highly recommend them as a source of information.[34]

Incidence of Abortion
- Nearly half of pregnancies among American women are unintended, and about four in ten of these are terminated by abortion.
- Twenty-two percent of all pregnancies (excluding miscarriages) end in abortion.
- Forty percent of pregnancies among white women, 67 percent among black women, and 53 percent among Hispanic women are unintended.
- In 2008, 1.21 million abortions were performed, down from 1.31 million in 2000. However, between 2005 and 2008, the long-term decline in abortions stalled.

Who Has Abortions?
- Eighteen percent of U.S. women obtaining abortions are teenagers. Those aged from fifteen to seventeen obtain 6 percent of all abortions, teens from age eighteen to nineteen obtain 11 percent, and teens younger than age fifteen obtain 0.4 percent.
- Women in their twenties account for more than half of all abortions. Women aged twenty to twenty-four obtain 33 percent of all abortions, and women aged twenty-five to twenty-nine obtain 24 percent.
- Non-Hispanic white women account for 36 percent of abortions, non-Hispanic black women 30 percent,

Hispanic women 25 percent, and women of other races 9 percent.
- Thirty-seven percent of women obtaining abortions identify as Protestant, and 28 percent identify as Catholic.
- Women who have never married and are not cohabiting account for 45 percent of all abortions.
- About 61 percent of abortions are obtained by women who have one or more children
- Forty-two percent of women obtaining abortions have incomes below 100 percent of the federal poverty level.
- Twenty-seven percent of women obtaining abortions have incomes between 100 and 199 percent of the federal poverty level.

How Do We Prevent Abortions?

Clearly the best way to reduce the use of abortion is to prevent unintended pregnancy.[35] Yes, letting people know about contraceptives and making them readily available is important, but it is not the only answer. We know that young people are less likely to become involved in sexual activity too soon if they have hope for the future and a good self-image. That applies to boys as well as girls. Major factors contributing to both hope for the future and a good self-image are learned before a child is three years old. Parents are the primary delivery source for these two factors, and when parents do not have hope for the future and good self-image, in most cases neither will the children. In the process of learning how to nurture their children, the parents receive nurturing also.

Most of the parents with whom I have had contact love their children and want them to succeed. They need the tools to make that happen. There are lots of programs available today. A group of churches, my own included, offered for several years, in partnership with our city and county health department, a program called Incredible Years.[36] The program provided hands-on training for parents. The church provided the space, child care, dinner, the lay coleader, and participant referrals from both our Child Development Center and our membership. The city and county provided the psychologist who led the training and made other referrals. Many of the participants had no relationship with our church before or after the training. Each group included about sixteen parents, with couples being highly encouraged to participate together. These classes, which lasted twelve weeks, included a cross section of humanity—middle class, working class, and the poor and several races. There was no charge to participants. The church even provided small door prizes to encourage attendance. This whole program cost the church about $2,000 for each series. In 2010 the state legislature in a cost-cutting move decided that the private partners in this program should pay the city and county health department for the participation of its staff. We could not afford to do so and shut the program down. Another program designed to help parents be parents is Parents as Teachers,[37] and there are others, but somebody has to care enough to get them funded and support them with his or her time and talents.

I track state legislation and did not know that the parenting training had been removed from the budget. It was no doubt a last-minute budget reduction "fix" implemented in a conference committee in the waning days of the legislative session. I did not even know such a reduction was being considered until I got the pre-pay bill from city and county just before we started the fall class. Yet I heard on the news, probably three or four times a day, updates throughout the legislative session on the bill that would require a woman to view an ultrasound of her baby before she could have an abortion.

We also need to provide structure for youth between the ages of twelve and sixteen after school and during school breaks. I love the Boys and Girls Club.[38] I also like the programs that take this age group and teach them preemployment life skills, thereby opening doors of new experiences and helping them discover talents and skills and explore where dreams and desires might lead them. Someday one of these kids could be on the team that finds the cure for cancer or diabetes, makes energy cleaner and less expensive, or negotiates peace in the Middle East. I would like it to be sooner than later for their sakes as well as ours.

Health Care

While changes made in preschool and middle school may impact the future, what remedial steps can we take to alleviate the problems of unwanted pregnancies among our young adults today? Readily available, preventive health care where the consequences of sexual behaviors are discussed might be a place to start. Young, healthy people do not normally go to the doctor unless they are very sick, injured, or pregnant. Before the passage of the Affordable Care Act, many regularly gambled with their health by not having health insurance.

A Living Wage Revisited

Do you see any correlations between abortions and what you read about the economy? Just look at two pieces of data again.

- Forty-two percent of women obtaining abortions have incomes below 100 percent of the federal poverty level

($10,830[39] in 2010 and $11,170 in 2012) for a single woman with no children.
- Twenty-seven percent of women obtaining abortions have incomes between 100 and 199 percent of the federal poverty level.

One of the byproducts of everyone earning a living wage, it appears, would be a reduction of abortions. This is not just a matter of money. It ties back to where we get our self-worth.

Human Sexuality

I am not an historian, but I love history and have informally wondered about where we Americans got our rather bizarre set of norms related to sexual behavior. We almost worship it. Actually, we probably do worship it in advertisement, media, and song, but we then rant and rave about our perceived notions of its misapplication. Are our views a catastrophic collision of our Puritan background and capitalism? That is the best explanation I can find. Two of the most divisive issues in the church today relate to sex: abortion and homosexuality. It seems to me that Jesus in his quest for the kingdom of God was most concerned about greed and misuse of power, but I suppose these both crop up in the misuse of sex.

The church needs to grapple with this question: how is our love of God and our love of our neighbor manifested in our sexual behavior? We need to dust off the teachings of Jesus and explore what they mean in the twenty-first century, not just reach back two thousand—or, more likely, six thousand—years and pick and choose among rules in the Bible that were developed on how the love of God and our neighbor was manifested in that time for those people. Certainly we do not need to start over. We can learn from our ancestors in the faith regarding how they lived out the way of God, but we have the obligation to learn from them, not enforce applications that were relevant when first developed and may still be relevant but may not. They, however, may be the example of a broader truth that still remains relevant but must be interpreted based on changes in culture. We did that very easily regarding polygamy and incest, which were normal parts of the nomadic lives of the Israelites, probably out of necessity, and faded from practice with improved lifestyles and scientific knowledge.

Sex is as essential to the continuation of humanity as eating. Like eating, God designed sex to be a pleasant and positive experience contributing to our health and well-being. And like eating we can misuse sex in as many ways as there are people on the earth. Do we live to eat, or do we eat to live? Is sex a means to an end or a means of expressing love?

At some point, particularly in the culture of the United States, sex somehow became a commodity rather than a means of expressing love or a desire for procreation. Actually, prostitution has been dubbed the oldest profession in the world. So I guess sex as a commodity has always existed. As the world has changed over the millennia, however, the need for people to be fruitful and multiply has decreased with industrialization and improved health conditions. Fewer people are now needed to harvest a crop or fight a war. More and more people are living to older and older ages. As a result, new paradigms have developed to define our sexual behaviors, leaning more toward an expression of love and fidelity than procreation.

Changes in society have also resulted in changing roles for men and women. If one really looks at the roles of women and men over the centuries, we see a pendulum of changing activities accompanying the development of society. Major changes resulted in times of societal dissonance. For example, during World War II, in general, men went to war and women went to work outside the home, and the good old days were gone for good.

We have seen these changes in church. In 1974, when I joined the church I now attend, elders and deacons were all men, and deaconesses were women who provided support for shut-ins. We had women serving in the role of Christian education director but none as ministers. Our first female elder was elected in the early 1980s, and female deacons were elected shortly thereafter. We still have deaconesses, and they are still all women, but the elders, both men and women, have taken on a larger role in addressing the spiritual needs of shut-ins. Since that time, we have had women and men serve at every level of leadership in our congregation, and most of the younger people have no idea it was ever any other way.

While pay is still very unequal between males and females, there are few jobs that women have not done, and there are more and more men entering fields that have been typically identified as jobs for women. I also see divisions of labor among young parents that are based on interest, time, and talent, not gender.

Marriage is no longer the only choice, particularly for women but also for men. Before the twentieth century, marriage often equaled survival. A widower with six children approached a widow with two children who had no means of support, and they married out of the need to raise the children and live. In many instances they grew to love each other.

Having children is also a choice for most adults, and both singles and married couples use adoption, artificial insemination, and surrogacy. In China the government has laws limiting the number of children each couple can have based on their individual circumstances. Abortion can become a tool for selecting certain traits, including gender.[40]

How do we love God and love our neighbor as we love ourselves at such a time as this? Overpopulation is a problem. Feeding the peoples of the world is a challenge. There are no easy answers. Yet God must believe in us, for it is God who is opening our eyes to see our neighbors at the homeless meeting, our neighbors in China, our childless neighbors longing to be parents, and our teenagers longing to be loved. God equips God's people when they are ready to rise to the occasion. It is time that we take "Rise up, Christian, and follow"[41] to heart. I can think of no better or bigger challenge than working toward a world where every child is wanted, welcomed, and nurtured. I can think of no better population to meet this challenge than the people who have chosen to follow the one who said, "Let the little children come to me, and do not stop them; for it is to such as these that the kingdom of heaven belongs."[42]

CHAPTER 14
THE ISSUES THAT DIVIDE US: GUNS

It is true that guns do not kill people; people kill people. In many instances, people kill people with guns. In many instances, the people who are killed are innocent bystanders, often children. Sometimes those people who kill people are children.

My grandfather's rifle hangs on the wall in my brother's house in a place of honor. I never knew this grandfather because he died when my dad was ten years old. The gun was special to my dad and is now special to my brother and actually to me also. The use of guns is a way of life in rural Oklahoma. I do not really remember my dad being much of a hunter, but he did hunt some, always, in my memory, in search of food. Rabbit and quail were the two things I remember most that we ate from the wild. Deer were not as abundant in the area where I lived when I was a child as they are now. All of my nephews and grandnephews and some of my grandnieces hunt and fish. They were trained to shoot well and accurately and to recognize that real guns are not toys. They have the appropriate licenses and hunt at the designated times. Actually, some of them also hunt with bow and arrows and black powder rifles. They eat what they kill or give the meat to someone else. There is a program where hunters can donate what they kill at various butcher shops that process it and pass it on to programs for the homeless. My dad did make it a point to shoot any rattlesnake or other poisonous snake he might happen upon, and he had a pistol that he used for this. We did not eat snakes, although I have eaten rattlesnake as an adult, and it was not bad. I have no doubt that my father or any of my other family members who use guns would use them to protect themselves or their families. While I do not do guns, I understand this way of life.

A few years ago, the news reported here in Oklahoma City that a toddler had been killed sleeping on the coach in the living room of the family's home. It seems a gang thought someone involved in another gang was in the house. The shooter killed the toddler while spraying the whole house with bullets from an automatic weapon. The toddler, I guess, should be considered collateral damage. Just as I have been writing this book, twelve people were killed in a similar fashion in a movie theater in Aurora, Colorado, with fifty-eight more injured, and seven were killed and three injured at a Sikh temple in Wisconsin.

The second amendment to the US Constitution sets the parameters regarding the legality of the use of guns. It states, "A well regulated militia, being necessary to the security of a free state, the right of the people to keep and bear arms, shall not be infringed." I do not think even Mrs. Gerhring, my seventh- and eighth-grade teacher, could diagram that sentence, and I certainly would not want to be the one to decide what it means. In 2008, with the Heller decision, the Supreme Court held, "The Second Amendment protects an individual right to possess a firearm unconnected with service in a militia, and to use that arm for traditionally lawful purposes, such as self-defense within the home."[43]

The ruling goes on to say that guns used for unlawful purposes can be limited. The question that is caught in the gap is this: how can the law be used to prevent the unlawful use of firearms? It does not help society a lot to know that a young man apparently suffering from mental illness killed twelve people and will most likely spend the rest of his life in prison or in a mental hospital because of it. There were warning signs. Appropriate authorities were concerned, but they had no grounds on which to act. What actions would be appropriate in a free and just society? It seems we consider only two very radical responses: do away with all guns or fully arm all people and let them protect themselves. Both ways brings us fully back to consideration of collateral damage, and neither will suffice.

Background checks for people purchasing guns makes sense but does not always catch the person who may have not yet been diagnosed with a mental illness. Licensure of gun owners, requiring proof of skill level like we do with driving, might curb the misuse of guns by untrained persons. Most deaths that result from guns, however, are not caused by people who are apt to get such a license. Requiring the registration of a title for a gun and a transfer of title when the gun is sold, given away, or inherited might keep guns out of the hands of people who should not have them. Educational campaigns alerting gun owners to safety precautions have probably helped keep guns out of the hands of children and should be continued. Control of the use of weapons designed for military action by amateurs seems wise. But if it is true that guns do not kill people and people kill people, does it not make sense to target our efforts at preventing people from killing people?

Mental Health Services

Does your state ration mental health care? If a child or adult is identified as needing some help in coping with the challenges of life, are services available for him or her? Most likely they are not. Governmentally sponsored mental health services are limited and rationed, and private mental health services are expensive. Such services have limited insurance coverage. For some mentally ill people, telling them they can see a mental health practitioner no more than sixteen or even sixty times a year is like telling an insulin-dependent diabetic that he or she can have sixteen or sixty doses of insulin a year. There is also a social stigma attached to receiving mental health care. Tell someone you are going in for a CAT scan to check out a possible tumor, and they will offer to pray for you and wish you luck. Tell someone you are seeing a psychiatrist, and they are likely to change the subject. The gun lobby has proved to be a powerful tool in getting progun legislation passed and killing antigun legislation. I would love to see that mighty force take aim at improving mental health services across this land.

Drug and Alcohol Abuse

It is impossible to address concerns about guns and their use without considering the link between gun use and drug or alcohol abuse. While we do need to continue our diligence in trying to stop the trafficking of drugs and people, we also need to reduce or eliminate the misuse of drugs and alcohol.

It is my understanding that one of the ploys used by the US government to "encourage" Indians to vacate their lands[44] in the east was to shut off most commerce to the areas belonging to the tribes. The one business that was allowed to flourish by the US government on Indian lands was the sale of alcoholic beverages. When the Cherokee were resettled in Oklahoma, the liquor business followed them. With little control over commerce, the tribe chose to dissuade drinking. For example, clubs were formed among its youth to help them understand that intoxication was a means of undercutting their futures. Are we working at all levels to address drug use and alcohol abuse? Is there a role for the church in addressing this problem? Have we explored well and addressed the connection between drugs, the underground economy, and poverty?

Early Intervention

Buried deep in the annals of the Great Society was a pilot program in which Oklahoma participated that was never implemented. It was a program to ensure that all children got an equal chance at success in life. The program created a link between public schools and human services to address the needs of children who met certain behavioral criteria. It was prevention at its best. A social worker would receive the referral and make a home visit to offer help to the family regarding the child's school issues. Receiving help was on a voluntary basis on the part of the parent. These were primarily early intervention contacts. In some instances the parents were experiencing similar issues with the child. In most instances the parents chose to receive help because they wanted the very best for their child. By all accounts this program was a shining success, but it was never funded after the pilot program was completed. A whole host of issues besides irresponsible use of guns could be prevented if such a program were readily available in schools, particularly those in high-risk areas. We have a wonderful, similar program in Oklahoma City called Positive Tomorrows[45] that targets the needs of homeless children, but such programs are too few and far between to meet the breadth of the need.

If you think prevention is too expensive, think again. How much is spent at all levels of government to address criminal behavior? How much does collateral damage cost in tax dollars? How much are we wasting in human equity among the people we ignore until they become a danger to themselves or others who could be making a valuable contribution to our society?

A Final Word Regarding Guns

A gun indeed is an inanimate object without the power of thought or action. It is thus not something in which we should put our faith. Neither is it a source of salvation. We have only one Savior, Jesus Christ, and only one God over whom we are not to place any other person or thing. We would do well to examine all things that may have pushed or be pushing their way into our hearts and minds above our one God. Regarding any weapon, we might want to remember the stories of Joshua,[46] Gideon,[47] and David and Goliath.[48] It seems in each of these stories God used what appears to be weakness to show God's strength. While we long for the time when we can beat our swords into plowshares,[49] we might want to hone our skills at loving our neighbor in preparation for that great day.

Christian Response

What is a Christian to do? How do we love God and love our neighbors in the midst of violence?

Children live behind the curtains along streets in many major cities where most of us would not drive our cars with the windows up and the doors locked. Veterans, some with disabilities, are seen regularly at food kitchens and in homeless shelters. They now have become collateral damage. Teenagers, even preteens, are abusing substances that can cause serious permanent damage with one use. While we deplore this when it is discussed regarding big cities, trust me, it has arrived in small towns too.

Churches can respond. Churches in safer communities can adopt a church in a challenged area. That can mean everything from designated donations to actual delivery of home-grown food to mission trips to working side by side with people trying to recover their neighborhoods. Many denominational groups have intercity mission programs that are designed to have groups come on work trips. Some question how much good can come from spending one week cleaning gutters or picking up trash or painting over graffiti. If nothing else, it opens the eyes of the person who is serving to the actual life situations of the neighbor they are called to love. It might also open our eyes to the existence of the same problems in our own backyard.

The Children's Defense Fund is a great resource for helping children with the challenges they face and what is being and can be done about them. I am particularly impressed with its annual call to observance of a Children's Sabbath, which my denomination precedes with Forty days of Prayer for Children. You might also check out its Cradle to Prison Pipeline campaign for more ideas.[50] Actually, its whole website is worth exploring.

Love is a verb. It requires action. It does not require you to do everything. It does require you to do something and do it well with all your heart, mind, soul, and strength. Perhaps God knew it would be easier to love some neighbors if we did it in groups. It sometimes is easier to obey Christ's admonition to fear not, when we have friends with us who are fearing not also. We call it the body of Christ.

CHAPTER 15
THE ISSUES THAT DIVIDE US: IMMIGRATION

Give me your tired, your poor, Your huddled masses yearning to breathe free; The wretched refuse of your teeming shore, Send these, the homeless, Tempest-tossed to me I lift my lamp beside the golden door!
—Inscription on the Statue of Liberty, from "The New Colossus" by Emma Lazarus

You shall also love the stranger, for you were strangers in the land of Egypt.
—Deuteronomy 10:19

Then the king will say to those at his right hand, "Come, you that are blessed by my Father, inherit the kingdom prepared for you from the foundation of the world; for I was hungry and you gave me food, I was thirsty and you gave me something to drink, I was a stranger and you welcomed me, I was naked and you gave me clothing, I was sick and you took care of me, I was in prison and you visited me
—Matthew 25:34–36

Our Declaration of Independence says that all men are created equal. We know now that that statement was assumed to mean only white men and clearly excludes women, but even with that, it was an amazingly progressive idea born from the struggles of the colonies to make some sense out of their political position in the world in 1776. It was a very new concept in a new world, but it was also a very old concept whose time for recognition had arrived. "There is no longer Jew or Greek, there is no longer slave or free, there is no longer male and female; for all of you are one in Christ Jesus" (Galatians 3:28).

There are no borders in the nation of God. Welcoming the stranger is described, commanded, and commended throughout the Bible. God's creation of humankind in God's own image irrevocably links all people as children of God whether we like it or not. As technology, transportation, and communication make the world smaller every day, those who are counted as strangers among us reduce in number and transition to neighbors. In either case, they are welcomed in the nation of God.

The world we live in does have borders and rules about those borders. Until we reach a point of equanimity, I fear it will always be so. How do citizens of the nation of God foster equanimity in whatever nation of this earth they may find themselves toward the end of borders no longer mattering?

All of my ancestors arrived in the United States before the Statue of Liberty was dedicated in 1886. I have not found when the first in a few of my lines arrived, but they were all here before 1850, most before 1790, when the first immigration laws were established. Three came from England, three from Germany, one from France, and one from Ireland. None as far as I know were famous, though one was potentially infamous. All seemed to have worked hard to pursue what is called the American dream—went to church, raised families, owned land, paid taxes, were counted in most censuses (although I cannot find William Knott in the 1800 census), and migrated from east to west, at least as far as Oklahoma. The earliest arriver so far that I have identified was John Daggett, who came in 1630. They all had to learn how to live with the natives who were already here for better and sometimes for worse. Most of them had family who fought on one side or the other of the Civil War. Some were involved with people who came here against their choice. I have a copy of the will where one of my great-grandparents left his house slaves to his children and a family picture that included the black nanny who had nowhere to go after the war. She migrated west with the family and lived out her life with them apparently by invitation and choice. Our country was founded, in general, on welcoming the stranger, even though we did not always get it right, have had to come back and revise a few things, and still have much more to do. This diversity is a good thing. Our language is now peppered with words from all around the world. We eat cuisine that represents every continent and in some cases combine and create new tastes from them. Our music, art, and literature are as diverse as our people.

The US Constitution, ratified on March 4, 1789, provided under the powers of Congress in section eight the power "to establish an uniform Rule of Naturalization, and uniform Laws on the subject of Bankruptcies throughout the United States." Congress quickly exercised its responsibility in 1790 by setting out statutes related to the naturalization of free white persons. I said we had to come back and revise a few things. I would also love to know why they combined immigration with bankruptcy, but that is for another time.

Our immigration laws are currently structured within a quota system by country of origin and in consideration of would-be immigrants' skills, profession, or relationship to family in the United States. Highly skilled professionals, for example, athletes, and scientists are considered in one classification, and laborers are in another. In both instances, someone needs to sponsor the aspiring immigrant before he or she can receive immigration papers. The process of applying for and receiving permission to legally immigrate is laborious, time consuming, and expensive—unless you are being cherry-picked to, say, play on a sports team or develop new computer software. Then it is amazing how fast paperwork can be processed.

If you are a picker of cherries or tomatoes or beans, your desirability is directly related to this year's crop and whether there is anyone in the United States willing and able to pick it when it needs to be picked. I suppose there are some who travel to, say, Mexico and interview potential employees before they plant their crops, and once they have chosen the workers, they begin planting. Somehow I do not think there are very many of those people. The United States needs a fast and efficient immigration system that allows the US government to develop and maintain listings of jobs in the country in which there are routinely worker shortages. Persons who are skilled in those jobs should then be able to apply for a temporary work visa and be vetted with background checks, etc. They could then present themselves to potential employers and work for the length of their work visas or go home if they are not hired.

Please be aware that I am not the first person who has thought of this rather simple solution. One of the problems with hiring a legal immigrant is that employers must offer them the same benefits as a US citizen. This suggests that the reason we do not "fix" our immigration laws is that we do not want to fix them.

Actually the same requirements exist for highly skilled professionals. I am certainly not an expert regarding immigration laws. What I report here is from my personal experience, and it is very possible that I got some of the rules wrong, because they are very convoluted. This highly skilled group, however, has an entry into the workforce because many of this category of people first arrive in the United States on educational visas. The educational visa has an internship or on-the-job experience proviso that allows a student to work as a part of his or her educational experience. The problem for the employer arises in this situation if the student wishes to continue in the employment at the end of the educational visa and must switch to a work visa. The work visa essentially requires that the employer make every effort to find a US citizen who meets the requirements for the job and hire them rather than the legal alien. Another requirement is that the employer must pay the legal alien at a fair rate for the job based on what is being paid for similar jobs in the general public.

The Oklahoma state government operates through a merit system where, for most jobs, individuals who apply for them must be preapproved as meeting the qualifications and in some cases tested and then ranked according to their qualifications. It is from each of these lists that agencies draw the top five or so names to interview for the job. When I was administering work requiring computer programming, there was rarely ever anyone on the list for programming positions. We had to go find people, often students, send them to get tested, and beat any other agency to them once their names were added to the list. State salaries are notoriously low, and in a couple of instances our salaries for computer programmers were below what had been determined to be the pay minimum for a specific job, so we could not even hire the students at times. When we did have them in a position with a salary that usually was just over the minimum and needed to switch them to a work visa, we had to advertise the position in the newspaper and prove that no citizen met the qualifications. I do not think I ever got a response to any of those job announcements.

Work visas are time limited. If the person who holds the work visa wants to remain in the United States, he or she must immediately start the application for a green card, which allows permanent residency and is the starting point for citizenship. While no one is required to hire an attorney to complete this process, it is highly recommended and expensive. My experience is limited to a few people, but I never had any get their green card within the time frame of the work visa. So the employer and the employee have to go through the process of getting an extension on the work visa.

I have no firsthand knowledge of how the immigration process proceeds regarding refugees, but I can imagine it being even more complicated. I do know that it took thirteen years for one of my friends to bring a relative to live with them because of the quota system.

Of course, in a perfect world, no one would have to leave their homeland to provide for his or her family or to avoid oppression, persecution, terror, and war. We do not live in a perfect world, and the nation of God and the nations of the world need to work together to ameliorate those situations that drive people from their homelands. In the United States and in every nation, adults need to earn a living wage, children should not have to work, and systems should exist to provide what we call a safety net for the elderly or disabled. Our success in being a blessing to other nations may be the most realistic solution to illegal immigration. It probably will not solve our scarcity of workers in some crucial jobs.

CHAPTER 16
THE ISSUES THAT DIVIDE US: HOMOSEXUALITY

> Justice is turned back, and righteousness stands at a distance; for truth stumbles in the public square, and uprightness cannot enter. Truth is lacking, and whoever turns from evil is despoiled. The Lord saw it, and it displeased [God] that there was no justice.
> —Isaiah 59:14–15

Whether two people of the same sex should be able to enter into the same type of contractual relationship as two people of the opposite sex resulting in special governmental acknowledgments and shortcuts is very simply a justice issue. Yes, they should be able to enter into the same type of contractual relationship. The simple solution, for the sake of justice, is to call all such contractual relationships, heterosexual or homosexual, civil unions. In some countries, the procurement of a governmentally issued license is simply the governmental acknowledgement of the contractual relationship. Marriage is left to churches.

So I guess the real question is who owns the word *marriage*. The church is certainly divided on this one. The truth is that some churches in the United States have been performing marriage ceremonies or covenant services for gay and lesbian couples for many years. Until recently, those marriages have not been recognized by the government and still are not in many states. I suppose that in and of itself is an example of the government establishing or at least enforcing a specific form of religion on people who do not share the belief.

I have to tell you, though; I think all heterosexuals owe a debt of gratitude to the homosexuals who have shined a light on what marriage is really all about. Marriage is not just about justice. Marriage is also about love and commitment and the public recognition of that bond. Justice can assure rights of property ownership and inheritance, rights to health insurance, rights to make medical decisions, and rights regarding children and child support. Certainly in our society these rights are important. But some gays and lesbians want society to accept them for who they are as individuals and as couples who consider the bonds of love sacred, not just a legal contract.

My first real encounter with someone who was gay was many years ago. I was just out of college. He was good-looking and fun. I was attracted to him. We ran around together like I ran around with my girlfriends—went out to eat on an impulse or to a movie. And I must tell you I rather enjoyed not having to deal with a guy who came on too strong too early in a relationship. I did, however, eventually begin to worry about what was wrong with me. I guess he sensed something was amiss because he finally told me that he was gay. Being the great "love people just the way they were" kind of person I was, I thanked him for being honest with me, and we continued as friends until various new jobs and moves separated us. I, however, did not sleep a wink the night he told me that he was gay. My head pounded the reality of what he had told me and what that meant about me. Of course, it did not mean anything about me. I, like many, I think, normally function within the mind-set that the world revolves around me.

It is always perplexing when I get slapped across the face with the reality that the world does not revolve around me.

People who are not like me need my mercy just as much as I need theirs, and we all need God's. And while I strive every day to love all people just the way they are, I still require the loving grace of God, who enables me to love all my neighbors as I would like to be loved, for the child of God I am and they, too, are. Alas, I am not perfect. I do have the need sometimes to determine my own worth by comparing myself to others. It never works, you know. I am not saying there is anything wrong with being competitive, but the person we each need to compete most against is him- or herself as we all strive for the perfection Paul talks about. We can learn from watching how other people succeed in the areas that challenge us, but improvement and growth come only with self-application. I thank God regularly that God's spirit is there to nudge me and sometimes slap me across the face to keep me on track.

This tendency among most of us to determine our own worth by using external mirrors is the source of much heartache and misjudgment. It shows up in our greed when we delude ourselves into thinking that just one more book (in my case) or the latest new electronic gadget or the best house on the block defines who or what we are. It shows up when we think the truth we know about God is the only truth about God. It shows up when we judge other people's behavior based only on what we know is right for ourselves. J. B. Phillips was right when he titled his now classic book *Your God Is Too Small*. God is big enough and strong enough and wise enough to let God's light shine through each of God's children made in God's image. Our task is to love God and love all our neighbors until we are no longer seeing dimly through a mirror.[51]

The challenge for the church and for each of us is to wrestle with that ever-present pull to judge others rather than love them. If you view marriage as a sacrament, as I do, then we have to let God own the institution of marriage. None of us can ever know the heart, mind, or soul of another like God can. God is the author of every marriage and indeed what God has joined together no human can separate. We judge others at our own peril, risking committing the sin of stepping into Christ's role as judge. Paul charges us in Philippians 2:12b–13 "to work out your own salvation with fear and trembling; for it is God who is at work in you, enabling you both to will and to work for his good pleasure." Paul does not say anything about working out someone else's salvation. In fact, Philippians 2 might be a good chapter to review every time we are tempted to step into the role as judge. God knows all God's children's hearts and minds and is constantly working with each of us to help us fully realize our full potential in the nation of God. That is true for both heterosexuals and homosexuals.

Self-Destructive Behavior

That being the case, we must still deal with the thorny issue of what our responsibility is toward our neighbors who appear to be involved in what we believe are self-destructive behaviors. First, I think we need to be very clear that what we think may be self-destructive, such as homosexual love and marriage, may not be. I am left handed and I am very glad that my parents did not accept the beliefs of their grandparents about left-handed people. I thought I was the only left-handed person on either side of my family until one of my older aunts assured me that two of my great-aunts had been left-handed. They were forced to use their right hand because being left-handed was considered to be evil.

I guess our ancestors thought they had biblical support for this belief, although the only mentions of being left-handed in the Bible are in Judges—first about a Benjamite who was appointed by God to be a deliverer for the Israelites[52] and another about a fight between the tribe of Benjamin, which had twenty-six thousand soldiers, of which seven hundred were left-handed stone throwers whom "every one could sling a stone at a hair, and not miss."[53] Would you not want to have one of those guys on your baseball team? They were fighting against the rest of the Israelites, four hundred thousand in number, and it took three mighty rushes by the four hundred thousand against the twenty-six thousand before they overtook them. While the scripture does say God was on the side of the rest of the Israelites in this battle, the mention of the seven hundred was probably included to say the four hundred thousand were going up against the best of the best when it came to pitching stones. Jesus' story of the cast-outs in Matthew 25 being placed on the left might have been the source of this connection of left-handedness with evil, but his visual picture was a common way of sorting things in other references in the Bible and was probably not casting dispersion on a minority group as we humans are wont to do. This will probably seem funny to some readers today. It was not funny to my great-great-grandmother when she discovered her daughters were so marked.

Second, while I do think there are times when direct intervention is essential (to prevent suicide, for example), it has been my experience that people do not change their behavior because someone else wants them to. It does help at times for people to learn about different or better ways to live. It certainly helps for someone to know they are loved no matter what. And it helps to have a friend walking with us as we exit the paths of greed, gluttony, promiscuity, adultery, or whatever else is preventing each of us from being in sync with God and becoming the person God created us to be.

Third, we need to remember we have an Advocate and a Savior who is ever present and able to hear our concerns and guide our steps when we spend time in prayer and meditation. I have found in many instances of my expressed concern for others, I am the one who God must change first before I can unselfishly be a conduit of God's healing love for my neighbor.

The Real Issue

The real issue regarding homosexuality or any of the other things that are tearing apart the body of Christ, however, has nothing to do with church and state, although it seems some Christians are trying to foster governmental action to give credence to their theological stances. This is a misuse of government and is an attempt to take Christians off the hook for actually grappling with the issue. For example, many church governance meetings at all levels have been torn asunder in recent years over homosexuality in general and homosexual marriage and ordination of homosexuals in particular. Why?

I know of no other way of life or behavior that is assigned by some churches such a horrendous stigma as homosexuality. If one believes it is a sin and therefore a reason for exclusion from the ministry and the church itself, then why do we not apply the same rule to, say, gluttony? As far as I can tell the church is guilty of being a downright codependent encourager of gluttony. The popular prosperity gospel seems to me to feed only our greed. Or how about adultery? Several years ago I served on a pulpit committee that was provided, among others, a candidate to consider who was documented as being guilty of adultery with not just one but two female members of two different churches. Why was he still on the list of available candidates? What about all the pastors and priests who sexually abused children and then moved to another ministry in another state? Adultery notwithstanding, it was my observation regarding the government that if it had been substantiated that a government employee had had sex or any other inappropriate behavior with a client, he or she was immediately fired. If that client was a minor, the employee was turned over to the judicial system for the prosecution of a crime. In both instances, the perpetrators also lost their professional credentials. But if you are homosexual, have loved God with all your heart, soul mind, and strength, loved your neighbor as yourself, and have lived in a loving, faithful relationship with the same partner for many years, you are not worthy to marry or be ordained. Really?

For some, the idea of homosexual behavior may just be repulsive, but we all have things that are repulsive to us that are not to others. My dad used to make me go into another room when I ate lemons in front of him. He said it made his teeth hurt, although he wore false teeth. I like okra just about any way it can be fixed, but I know lots of people who can eat it fried but never boiled. They say boiled okra is too slimy. I don't know of anyone yet being forbidden church participation because they ate lemons or slimy okra.

There are those who believe strongly that practicing homosexuality breaks Mosaic law, but if we eat catfish or pork or wear clothing made from two different fabrics, we are breaking Mosaic law.

Or is it possible that we are in need of a scapegoat—that we cannot fully accept that God loved us so much that God sent Jesus to end the need for a scapegoat? If that is the case, then we need to explore the whole idea of the scapegoat more thoroughly.

The concept of a scapegoat is biblical. It is described in Leviticus 16 as a remarkable and beautiful service of worship. What is presented in Leviticus is a far cry from our modern interpretation of this word. Merriam-Webster illustrates this difference very precisely, defining *scapegoat* as "a goat upon whose head are symbolically placed the sins of the people after which he is sent into the wilderness in the biblical ceremony for Yom Kippur," "one that bears the blame for others," or "one that is the object of *irrational hostility*" (emphasis mine).[54]

In Leviticus 16, you will see that first Aaron, the priest, after cleansing himself and dressing appropriately, entered the sanctuary with a bull for a sin offering for himself, two goats for a sin offering for the people of Israel, and one ram for a burnt offering. He offers the bull for a sin offering for himself and makes atonement for himself and his household. He then takes the two goats to the entrance of the meeting tent and cast lots to determine which of the goats is to be offered as a sin offering to make atonement for the people. Finally, he takes the remaining goat and, laying his hands on its head, confesses all the iniquities of the people of Israel and sends the goat away into the wilderness. The Day of Atonement continues today to be one of the High Holy Days in the Jewish faith observed each fall.

There are two things I want to call to our attention. First is the need for the priest to offer the bull for his and his family's atonement and one goat for all of Israel. There is a message in that practice. Perhaps Jesus stated that message most succinctly in Matthew 7 when he cautioned us against judging others, asking,

> Why do you see the speck in your neighbor's eye, but do not notice the log in your own eye? Or how can you say to your neighbor, "Let me take the speck out of your eye," while the log is in your own eye? You hypocrite, first take the log out of your own eye, and then you will see clearly to take the speck out of your neighbor's eye.[55]

Second, note what Aaron does in the story regarding the "scapegoat." He does not pass judgment on the people; he merely acts as a conduit for the people, letting their sins go away from them and removing a barrier that separates them from God. The goat had to be without blemish when it was selected for use at the altar; it was not changed in this process, but rather used as a beast of burden, if you will, to carry away those things that served as impediments to a relationship with God.

As Christians, our atonement was accomplished on a cross as the Son of God faced down evil for good. While we, I believe, must be ever vigilant of those logs that can accumulate in our eyes and accept God's cleansing forgivingness, our being one with God was given as grace to us through God's Son. There is no us and them in regard to God's love. Our salvation is not conditioned on our being more or less righteous than another. We are relieved of the burden of practicing irrational hostility toward anyone. In fact, such attitudes and behaviors form a barrier between us and others, short-circuiting our ability to love them as God has called us to do.

I spoke earlier about cultural Christianity and how taking things out of context results in very interesting theology. We were discussing something similar to this in my Sunday school class recently, and one member stated that from childhood she had thought "cleanliness is next to godliness" was from the Bible. At some point she looked it up, and lo and behold, it was not there! How often do we project our own philosophies onto God without realizing it? And how adept are we at sorting out what is our own philosophy and what is God's?

While we may long for something or someone else to blame for our own shortcomings and we may feel a little better about ourselves if we can feel hostility toward someone we think is not as righteous as we are, we will not find either to ever be appropriate behavior in the nation of God. We are called to work diligently to stay in sync with God and to be in a constant state of reconciliation with God through Christ. And likewise, we must follow a pattern of reconciliation, with God's help, with all of God's children, for they are our neighbors whom we are called to love. There is one table from which God's abundance flows without concern for righteousness or gluttony, as far as that's concerned. It is Lord 's Table, and it offers us reconciliation each time we come there to dine.

CHAPTER 17
HEAR THE CALL

Remember the story of twelve-year-old Jesus making the annual trip to the temple.[56] He was so awe inspired that he lost track of time and failed to join the caravan for its trip home. Many of us can harken back to a time when God's presence was just as palpable. We long for those times and feelings. Many of us relate it to certain music and special mentors and think that if we could just recapture that, all would be well.

But all is not well. The world seems to be spinning out of our control. Even the music and the mentors are alien to us. Where we should be able to fine oneness in Christ, where we should reconnect with God and gain synergy from sharing with our brothers and sisters in Christ, we fight with one another—the music is too loud or boring or out-of-date; we need to add video or other technology or not; we debate whether to keep old gothic buildings or open coffee shops; we seem to think that conservative or liberal theology or, worse yet, politics hold the key to control. It is all pretty trivial, all too human, I fear, when it comes right down to it.

What do you think the test of time will say about those more serious sticky-wicket issues that burn our time and energy as we argue about who is right and who is wrong without a lot of concern for who is being left out? How much closer do you think we will be to the nation of God and being one in God as a result of all that effort?

Because we are living longer now, we have five even six generations worshiping together in our churches. Never before in the history of the church have that many sets of taste in music, styles of worship, or understandings of faith comingled. In the United States and in many other parts of the world, we have citizens representing every religion, culture, race, and ethnicity. What feels like a world that is spinning out of our control may be the continuing plan of God to make us one. If that is the case, would it not be more productive to invest our energies in reaching out to the one who is in control? Would it not be a wonderful gift to God if God's people obeyed God and loved our way into oneness rather than fought our way out of it?

Now compare the story of Jesus' childhood visit to the temple to his final trip to Jerusalem when he wept over his people, saying,

> If you, even you, had only recognized on this day the things that make for peace! But now they are hidden from your eyes. Indeed, the days will come upon you, when your enemies will set up ramparts around you and surround you, and hem you in on every side. They will crush you to the ground, you and your children within you, and they will not leave within you one stone upon another; because you did not recognize the time of your visitation from God. (Luke 19:41–44)

Is Jesus saying something similar to the church today? I rather think he is. Luke was most likely written around the time the Jews were facing the destruction of the temple in Jerusalem toward the close of the first century. At that time, Christianity was one of many sects within Judaism. Were these various groups spending more of their time and resources proving who was right and who was wrong rather than investing it in following God's commands to love? Did their divisions weaken them and prove to at least be a part of the reason the Romans were able to overthrow them? Was their failure to be a blessing to all nations another factor?

Our response to Jesus' call to love God and love one another is more important than anything else. How can we turn our backs on following Jesus' example? How can we stubbornly follow our own way when we know what happened after his time of weeping: the cleansing of the temple, the Last Supper, the crucifixion, the resurrection, and the coming of the Holy Spirit? He took on evil and won. It does not get any better than that, people. All he asks of us is to love God and to love our neighbors as we love ourselves. Yet I believe he is weeping for us. We can turn around and go Christ's way. I take great heart in the phrase above: "If you, even you, had only recognized on this day the things that make for peace!" The only proof we can offer that we recognize the things that make for peace is to live them.

I must confess when reading the story of God's call to Mary to be the mother of Christ; I have wondered if there were other young women God had approached before finding one who said, "Yes". How many never heard the call because they were not listening for God? How many never heard the call because they were too distracted, perhaps even at the temple? How many heard the call but thought, "Surely God does not want me to do that?" How many heard the call but were afraid to say yes?

The command to love God and to love our neighbors as we love ourselves was issued some four thousand plus years ago. The call to oneness was made two thousand plus years ago. Do we Christians of the twenty-first century hear the call? Are we ready like Mary to say, "Here am I, the servant of the Lord; let it be with me according to your word" (Luke 1:38)? We are not a lone, young woman, but a whole body of people sharing the call at this time in the nation of God. God is calling us. Trust God. God is saying to us, "It's about time. Let's go. I'm with you."

AFTERWORD

The book of Revelation talks about the church being the bride of God when it describes the ultimate nation of God—that state toward which all our energies as individual Christians and as communities of faith are targeted. Perhaps if we searched deeply into this imagery we might gain insight regarding what God is actually calling us to.

> Then I saw a new heaven and a new earth; for the first heaven and the first earth had passed away, and the sea was no more. And I saw the holy city, the new Jerusalem, coming down out of heaven from God, prepared as a bride adorned for her husband. And I heard a loud voice from the throne saying, "See, the home of God is among mortals. He will dwell with them; they will be his peoples, and God himself will be with them; he will wipe every tear from their eyes. Death will be no more; mourning and crying and pain will be no more, for the first things have passed away." (Revelation 21:1–4)

Have you ever known anyone who actually seemed happiest when they were in misery? Do you think they will be satisfied in the nation of God described above? I heard a sermon recently addressing whether everybody will get to heaven. If we assume that every Christian will, I think the real question we need to deal with becomes this: do we really want to live in a nation that functions within the rule of love, God's love, with God sitting right there, every day, all the time in absolute transparency? Is this the one to whom we really want to be married? If we have spent our lives judging others, deluding ourselves in what is right and wrong for ourselves, or tearing down others to build ourselves up, I think that when we arrive in heaven we will at least experience some major culture shock and at worst think we are in hell.

Jesus' way is to start living as a citizen of the nation of God right now and every day forward. I believe that if we love God and love our neighbors as ourselves, eternity will take care of itself. The last words my mother said to me still ring in my ears.

"I want to go home."

Don't we all?

Little children, let us love, not in word or speech, but in truth and action.

—1 John 3:18

ENDNOTES

1. All scriptures quoted may be found in *The New Interpreter's Study Bible: New Revised Standard Version with the Apocrypha* (Nashville: Abingdon Press, 2003).
2. The New Interpreter's Study Bible (Nashville: Abingdon Press, 2003), 2035.
3. From the foreword to The Pogo Papers, Copyright 1952–53.
4. The story of wandering in the wilderness can be found in Exodus. Psalm 73 is a summarized, poetic version that also might be helpful. Both can be found in the Old Testament of any Bible.
5. "Where Is Love?" Words and Music by Lionel Bart from the Movie Oliver, 1960.
6. "Are You Able Said the Master." Words by Earl B. Marlatt, 1926; music by Harry S. Mason, Beacon Hill, 1924.
7. M. Scott Peck, M.D., The Road Less Traveled (New York: Simon and Schuster, 1978), 81.
8. Fred B. Craddock, Overhearing The Gospel (Christian Board of Publication, 2002).
9. My favorite easy-access book regarding the love of God. James Bryan Smith, Embracing the Love of God: The Path and Promise of Christian (HarperCollins Publishers, 2008).
10. Shelly Tochluk, Witnessing Whiteness: The Need to Talk About Race and How to Do It (Rowman & Littlefield Publishers, 2010).
11. Helen Keller, My Religion (Literary Licensing, LLC).
12. See Luke 15:11–32.
13. Kittel, Gerhard and Friedrich, Gerhard, editors; Geoffrey W. Bromley, translator; Theological Dictionary of the New Testament Abridged in One Volume (Grand Rapids: Eerdmans Publishing Company, 44).

14. Leviticus 18:22: "You shall not lie with a male as with a woman; it is an abomination."
15. Leviticus 20:13: "If a man lies with a male as with a woman, both of them have committed an abomination; they shall be put to death; their blood is upon them."
16. Pamela Eisenbaum is the author of Paul Was Not a Christian: The Original Message of a Misunderstood Apostle, (HarperCollins Publishers, 2010). At this writing she is associate professor of biblical studies and Christian origins at Iliff School of Theology in Denver, Colorado. She is also a practicing Jew.
17. Kittel and Friedrich, Theological Dictionary of the New Testament Abridged in One Volume, 47.
18. Jaclyn Cosgrove, "West Nile virus harder to understand, combat in Oklahoma because of funding cut," Oklahoman, September 1, 2012, http://newsok.com/west-nile-virus-harder-to-understand-combat-in-oklahoma-because-of-funding-cut/article/3706106.
19. Such continuums probably exist in all areas of government. Assuring the general welfare of our population is the area I know most about, so that is the area I am developing here.
20. http://www.merriam-webster.com/dictionary/just
21. http://www.theworldcafe.com/
22. Be assured the blood was not wasted; I strongly support blood donation at all times even when there is no crisis.
23. Timothy McVeigh was the man found guilty of the bombing.
24. Steven Kellogg, Chicken Little (HarperCollins Publishers, 1987).
25. http://www.aec.gov.au/faqs/voting_australia.htm
26. To see a living wage calculator, go to http://livingwage.mit.edu.
27. I use the familiar term "food stamps" throughout. The current formal name of the program as of 2012 was Supplemental Nutrition Assistance Program (SNAP).
28. "In 1965, U.S. CEOs in major companies earned 24 times more than an average worker; this ratio grew to 35 in 1978 and to 71 in 1989. The ratio surged in the 1990s and hit 300

at the end of the recovery in 2000. The fall in the stock market reduced CEO stock-related pay (e.g., options) causing CEO pay to moderate to 143 times that of an average worker in 2002. Since then, however, CEO pay has exploded and by 2005 the average CEO was paid $10,982,000 a year, or 262 times that of an average worker ($41,861)." http://www.epi.org/publication/webfeatures_snapshots_20060621/

29. "Squeezed by rising living costs, a record number of Americans, almost 1 in 2, have fallen into poverty or are scraping by on earnings that classify them as low income. The latest census data depict a middle class that is shrinking as unemployment stays high and the government's safety net frays. The new numbers follow years of stagnating wages for the middle class that have hurt millions of workers and families.'Safety net programs such as food stamps and tax credits kept poverty from rising even higher in 2010, but for many low-income families with work-related and medical expenses, they are considered too "rich" to qualify,' said Sheldon Danziger, a University of Michigan public policy professor who specializes in poverty." http://www.usatoday.com/news/nation/story/2011-12-15/poor-census-low-income/51944034/1

30. Hans Christian Andersen, The Emperor's New Clothes (Houghton Mifflin Harcourt, 2008).

31. http://www.naeyc.org/files/yc/file/201111/Rosie_the_Riveters_Children_Online_1111.pdf

32. Ruby K. Payne, Ph.D., Philip E. DeVol, and Terie Dreussi-Smith, Bridges Out of Poverty: Strategies for Professionals and Communities (aha Process Inc, 2011). See also http://www.bridgesoutofpoverty.com.

33. See the story in Second Kings 22.

34. http://www.guttmacher.org/sections/abortion.php?pub=sheets

35. http://www.nytimes.com/aponline/2012/10/05/health/ap-us-med-healthbeat-free-birth-control.html?_r=1&ref=aponline

36. http://www.incredibleyears.com/

37. http://www.parentsasteachers.org/
38. http://www.bgca.org/Pages/index.aspx
39. aspe.hhs.gov/poverty
40. http://geography.about.com/od/populationgeography/a/onechild.htm
41. Adapted from the old Negro spiritual "Rise Up, Shepherd, and Follow," which tells the story of the shepherds responding to the angels' announcement of the birth of Christ.
42. Matthew 19:14.
43. http://www.scotusblog.com/wp-content/uploads/2008/06/07-290.pdf
44. The story of the Indian removal from the east coast as recorded by Grant Foreman is online in two books: Indian Removal: The Emigration of the Five Civilized Tribes of Indians, located at http://books.google.com/books?id=L8ZOg03I0s0C&source=gbs_similarbooks, and The Five Civilized Tribes: Cherokee, Chickasaw, Choctaw, Creek, Seminole at http://books.google.com/books?id=II9_QT9MGbQC&source=gbs_similarbooks.
45. http://www.positivetomorrows.org/
46. Joshua 6.
47. Judges 7.
48. 1 Samuel 17.
49. Isaiah 2:4.
50. http://www.childrensdefense.org/programs-campaigns/cradle-to-prison-pipeline/
51. "For now we see in a mirror, dimly, but then we will see face to face. Now I know only in part; then I will know fully, even as I have been fully known" (1 Corinthians 13:12).
52. Judges 3:15.
53. Judges 20:16.
54. http://www.merriam-webster.com/dictionary/scapegoat
55. Matthew 7:3–5.
56. Luke 2:41–52.

CPSIA information can be obtained
at www.ICGtesting.com
Printed in the USA
FFOW05n0149020114